Euripides: *Cyclops*

COMPANIONS TO GREEK AND ROMAN TRAGEDY

Series Editor: Thomas Harrison

Aeschylus: Agamemnon Barbara Goward
Aeschylus: Eumenides Robin Mitchell-Boyask
Aeschylus: Persians David Rosenbloom
Aeschylus: Prometheus Bound I. A. Ruffell
Aeschylus: Seven Against Thebes Isabelle Torrance
Aeschylus: Suppliants Thalia Papadopoulou
Euripides: Alcestis Niall W. Slater
Euripides: Bacchae Sophie Mills
Euripides Cyclops Carl A. Shaw
Euripides: Hecuba Helene P. Foley
Euripides: Heracles Emma Griffiths
Euripides: Hippolytus Sophie Mills
Euripides: Ion Lorna Swift
Euripides: Iphigenia at Aulis Pantelis Michelakis
Euripides: Medea William Allan
Euripides: Orestes Matthew Wright
Euripides: Phoenician Women Thalia Papadopoulou
Euripides: Suppliant Women Ian Storey
Euripides: Trojan Women Barbara Goff
Seneca: Hercules Furens Neil W. Bernstein
Seneca: Phaedra Roland Mayer
Seneca Oedipus Susanna Braund
Seneca: Thyestes Peter Davis
Sophocles: Antigone Douglas Cairns
Sophocles: Ajax Jon Hesk
Sophocles: Electra Michael Lloyd
Sophocles: Oedipus at Colonus Adrian Kelly
Sophocles: Philoctetes Hanna Roisman
Sophocles: Women of Trachis Brad Levett

Euripides: *Cyclops*

A Satyr Play

Carl A. Shaw

BLOOMSBURY ACADEMIC
LONDON • NEW YORK • OXFORD • NEW DELHI • SYDNEY

BLOOMSBURY ACADEMIC
Bloomsbury Publishing Plc
50 Bedford Square, London, WC1B 3DP, UK
1385 Broadway, New York, NY 10018, USA

BLOOMSBURY, BLOOMSBURY ACADEMIC and the Diana logo
are trademarks of Bloomsbury Publishing Plc

First published 2018
Paperback edition first published 2019

Cover design: Terry Woodley
Cover image © akg-images/Erich Lessing

A catalogue record for this book is available from the British Library.

Library of Congress Cataloging-in-Publication Data
Names: Shaw, Carl A., author.
Title: Euripides, Cyclops : a satyr play / Carl A. Shaw.
Other titles: Companions to Greek and Roman tragedy.
Description: London ; New York : Bloomsbury Academic, 2018. |
Series: Companions to Greek and Roman tragedy |
Includes bibliographical references and index.
Identifiers: LCCN 2017045517 | ISBN 9781474245791 (hb) |
ISBN 9781474245814 (epub)
Subjects: LCSH: Euripides. Cyclops. | Greek drama (Satyr play)–History
and criticism. | Cyclopes (Greek mythology) in literature.
Classification: LCC PA3973.C9 S53 2018 | DDC 882/.01–dc23
LC record available at https://lccn.loc.gov/2017045517

ISBN: HB: 978-1-4742-4579-1
PB: 978-1-4742-4580-7
ePDF: 978-1-4742-4582-1
ePub: 978-1-4742-4581-4

Typeset by Integra Software Services Pvt. Ltd.

To find out more about our authors and books visit
www.bloomsbury.com and sign up for our newsletters.

For Amber and Elia

Contents

Figures

Preface

Although I have spent the last decade working on satyr drama, I always preferred the fragments of satyr plays to the *Cyclops*. A few years ago, I probably would even have traded Euripides' satyr play for any of Sophocles' or Aeschylus' lost satyric productions. But after spending a year with the *Cyclops*, analysing it and thinking about it, I truly believe what I wrote in this book's final paragraph: 'Euripides' *Cyclops* thrives under the burden of being its genre's only extant representative.' The play may lack some of the spectacular performative elements that appeared in other fifth- and fourth-century satyr plays, but it is much more sophisticated than it appears. At nearly every turn, Euripides presents a nuanced and playful reference to the theatre, satyr drama, religion, history, philosophy, or mythology. I am convinced that there is still much more to learn about the play.

Many people assisted in various ways during the process of writing this book. I owe thanks to the series editor, Tom Harrison, for trusting me to write about a satyr play in a series on Greek and Roman Tragedy. The team at Bloomsbury has been very helpful throughout the process, especially Alice Wright, Lucy Carroll, and Clara Herberg. I particularly appreciate the constructive and thoughtful criticism of the Bloomsbury readers. David Rohrbacher worked through the entire manuscript at a critical time and made numerous valuable suggestions, both at the small and large scale. Tricia Chua, Evan Giomi, Bill Kingdon, Tyler Kirby, and Dirk Warner were kind enough to read the *Cyclops* with me in our Advanced Greek class. The funding I received from the Loeb Classical Library Fellowship and the National Endowment for the Humanities (although granted for a separate project) was instrumental in helping me formulate much of this book. The Humanities Division at New College of Florida kindly covered costs for images. And my family and friends were, as always, indispensable throughout the entire process. Amber and Elia, in particular, were my inspiration. <4.

Notes for the Reader

1. All dates are BCE, unless otherwise noted.
2. Unattributed translations are my own.
3. Unless otherwise noted, Greek and Latin texts come from the most recent version of the Loeb Classical Library.

List of Abbreviations

FGrH	Die Fragmente der griechischen Historiker, ed. F. Jacoby. Berlin, 1923–1958.
IG II²	*Inscriptiones Graecae: Inscriptiones Atticae Euclidis anno posteriores*, 2nd edn. Berlin, 1913–1940.
IG Urb. Rom.	Moretti, Luigi. *Inscriptiones Graecae Urbis Romae*, 4 vols. in 5 parts. Rome, 1968–1990.
K-A	Kassel, R. and C. Austin. Poetae comici Graeci. Berlin, 1983–.
KPS	Krumeich, R., N. Pechstein, and B. Seidensticker. Das griechische *Satyrspiel*. Darmstadt, 1999.
LSJ	Liddel, H. G. and R. Scott. *A Greek-English Lexicon*, 9th edn., rev. H. S. Jones and R. MacKenzie, and suppl. P. G. W. Glare. Oxford, 1996.
TrGF	Kannicht, R., S. Radt, and B. Snell, *Tragicorum Graecorum fragmenta*, vols. I–V. Göttingen, 1971–2004.

The *Cyclops* and Satyr Drama

Introduction

Each year in Athens around the end of March, Athenians hosted a large festival, the City Dionysia, or Great Dionysia, in honour of the god Dionysus.[1] Ancient tradition states that it was founded to commemorate the events surrounding the city of Eleutherae's integration with Attica, the region around Athens.[2] The people of Eleutherae had offered the Athenians a statue of Dionysus in recognition of their new alliance, but the Athenians refused it, and in response Dionysus sent a plague that 'affected' the genitalia of all male citizens.[3] The divine affliction was cured only when the people of Athens received and recognized the cult of Dionysus in their city. These events were remembered and celebrated each year at the start of the City Dionysia with the phallophoria, a procession of citizens, metics (resident aliens), and delegates from Athenian colonies.[4] As these men paraded from outside the city towards the god's temple, they carried a wooden statue representing Dionysus, along with various bronze and wooden phallic icons. After making sacrifices at the sanctuary, they brought the idol into the theatre, where it resided during the most celebrated part of the festival, the theatrical performances.

Many details surrounding the City Dionysia remain murky, but its main theatrical components during most of the classical period are clear: each year there were twenty dithyrambs, three to five comedies, and three tragic tetralogies.[5] Dithyramb, the most poorly attested of the genres, was a massive civic and religious competition that involved more than one thousand citizens.[6] Each of the ten tribes of Attica submitted a chorus of fifty men and a chorus of fifty boys to dance and sing a hymn in honour of the god Dionysus. Comedy, which is preserved primarily in the works of Aristophanes and the fragmentary plays of Menander, was a single-day contest between three to five comic poets, all of whom staged their plays back to back.[7] Tragedy, though, was unique. Each of three playwrights was granted an entire day to stage a trilogy of tragedies followed by a satyr play, a humorous production with a chorus of playful half-man, half-horse creatures.[8]

Of the hundreds of satyr plays performed in ancient Greece, and of the forty-four surviving Greek theatrical productions (thirty-two tragedies and eleven comedies), Euripides' *Cyclops* is the only complete, extant example of ancient Greek satyr drama.[9] It is not, though, our only evidence. Papyrus fragments, quotes from ancient authors, inscriptional records, comments from ancient literary critics, and numerous satyr vases help provide a reasonable sense of the genre in its various stages. It is impossible to capture all phases of satyr drama's development in a single definition, but François Lissarrague offers a particularly helpful recipe for understanding fifth-century satyr play: 'Take one myth, add satyrs, observe the result.'[10] As Lissarrague's formula suggests, poets of classical satyr drama seem to have invariably staged an adaptation of a traditional mythological story.[11] However, they added a chorus of satyrs who had played no role in the original myth, thereby altering the entire character of the story, transforming it into a mythological burlesque. This chapter will provide the necessary context for understanding Euripides' fifth-century *Cyclops*, detailing the complex and ambiguous nature of satyrs, the history and functions of the genre, the Homeric model on which the play was based, and the date and history of the text.

Satyrs

Although satyrs are the central and necessary element of all ancient satyr drama, they remain somewhat enigmatic.[12] They are complex figures in appearance, in religious and cultural significance, and in historical development. Formally human in their upper half and equine in the lower, they vary in their degree of humanness and beastliness in ancient visual representations.[13] They were generally depicted with human feet, but could also have horses' hooves, especially in early archaic depictions, and they were traditionally portrayed with an erect, horse-sized phallus, but could also have a more human-sized member.[14] They first began to appear on vases in Greece around 580, and they became very popular around 560, but Hesiod is the earliest known poet to mention satyrs in literature, dubbing them 'worthless and mischievous'.[15] This description follows them through over a millennium of depictions in the Greco-Roman world, where they are consistently portrayed as wine-obsessed, sex-obsessed, lying, gluttonous cowards.

Despite their 'worthless' nature, satyrs are also distinguished in the Greek imagination as complex, divine, even philosophical in their character.[16] They are companions of the god Dionysus, and they travel with him, sharing in his revelries of dance, song, and drink. Silenus, the elderly father of the chorus of satyrs, is even depicted as the guardian of the baby Dionysus on various vases and in at least two satyr plays.[17] There is also a famous story about Silenus' capture by King Midas, which reflects a darker, philosophical element to the satyr. In a garden in Macedonia, Midas hunted and caught Silenus by filling a spring with wine. The satyr, who could not resist the drink, approached the pool of wine and consumed it all. When he passed out, the king captured him and asked him the secret to life, to which the satyr responded:

> Why are you forcing me to say things that are better for you not to know? Life is least sorrowful when you are ignorant of your own misfortunes. The best thing for humankind is to not be born at all … It is best for all men and all women never to exist; however, after this option, the next best thing to for humans is, once you are born, to die as quickly as possible.[18]

Silenus' response that the best thing for humans is to have never been born provides a bleak outlook on human life, but the most remarkable aspect about the sentiment is that it is spoken by a lecherous, wine-guzzling coward. Silenus, like all satyrs, is somehow both more animal than man, but also more divine.

As in their divinity and philosophical nature, satyrs defy clear categorization in their name and physical form. While the Greeks of the eastern Attic and Ionian regions called them satyrs (*saturoi*), the Peloponnesians referred to them as silens (*silenoi*), a term retained in the name of the satyrs' father figure, Silenus.[19] The *Homeric Hymn to Aphrodite* mentions silens (vv. 262–3) as the lovers of nymphs, and the artist of the François Vase (Figure 1.1) explicitly labels the half-horse, half-human creatures *silenoi*. At some point in the sixth century, satyrs and silens were merged and served as a single unit in Dionysus' *thiasos*, or ritual band of revelers, but physically their depictions continued to evolve. The François Vase, which presents the popular myth of Hephaestus' return to Mount Olympus, clearly demonstrates the horse- or ass-like qualities of archaic satyrs and silens.[20] They have horse legs and hooves, a long tail, thick equine thighs, and a large phallus that mirrors the horse on which Hephaestus rides. Above the waist, though, the *silenoi* are nearly indistinguishable from human or divine characters.

During the transition from the archaic to the early Classical period, illustrations of satyrs evolved to be more human. An Attic black-figure amphora from around 540, known as the Berlin Knights (Figure 1.2), even depicts one satyr with horse hooves, while the other three have human legs and feet. As the performative aspects of this vase suggest,

Figure 1.1 Hephaestus on a mule followed by a silen or satyr carrying a wineskin. Detail from the François Vase, Attic black-figure volute crater, *c.* 570 BCE. Museo archeologico nazionale di Firenze. Courtesy: Egisto Sani.

Figure 1.2 Silen and satyr/nymph chorus, Attic black-figure amphora, *c.* 540. Berlin Painter. Inv. F 1697. Photo: Johannes Laurentius. Antikensammlung, Staatliche Museen, Berlin, Germany/Art Resource, NY.

the progression from more horse-like to more human is probably due in large part to the popularity of satyrs (and dressing up as satyrs) in ritual performances.[21] Certain late archaic Attic vases clearly depict satyrs in Athenian processions, sometimes as an oversized figure being paraded through the city (e.g. Figure 1.3), and other times as a costumed individual riding in a ship cart with Dionysus (Figure 1.4). Later, Plato (*Leg.* 815c) even mentions men dressed as satyrs in the context of religious initiation.

Above all, then, satyrs were creatures of ambiguous nature. They were cowardly beasts with outsized appetites for sex, wine, dance, and song. In this way, they were more base than humans, but they also exceeded the capabilities of humankind. Dionysus considered them suitable companions in his many divine adventures, and they held a surprising philosophical role in ancient myth and legend.[22] Silenus is sometimes described as Dionysus' teacher (a rather ridiculous idea when looking at his role in the *Cyclops*), and King Midas believed Silenus knew the meaning of life. The extraordinary bleakness of the satyr's response eclipses some of its 'satyric' quality, but a closer examination reveals undeniable philosophical gravity and humour. Within the grim sentiment that death is greater than life, Silenus wraps a playful message of hope: whatever challenges one faces now are the worst that he or she will ever encounter. With death comes comfort and release from suffering in some form of life outside of life. In Greek art, religion, philosophy, and performance, Silenus and the satyrs prove that they are not simply subhuman or superhuman. They are free from the restraints of civilization, and their bestial and divine natures combine to make them somehow extra-human.

Satyr drama, the genre

Satyr drama shared a number of theatrical elements with both tragedy and comedy: it was performed on the same stage during the same festival, and used similar actors, chorus, musical instruments, masks, singing, and dancing. Formally, however, satyr drama was most closely related to tragedy.[23] It was written by tragedians, and it had an important role in the tragic competition, since it was the final performance before judging took place. Also, the same actors and choreuts who had performed in the trilogy of tragedies performed in the successive satyr play, and non-satyric characters dressed in the same tragic costumes and used the same language, meter, movement, and gestures. Satyr drama exhibits so many overlapping formal associations with tragedy that modern scholars sometimes find it challenging to decide whether an ancient fragment comes from a tragedy or a satyr play.[24] This was not the case, however, when the productions were originally performed, since the chorus of satyrs ensured that audiences could never mistake a satyr play for a tragic performance – satyrs were never used in tragedy.

Satyr drama's relationship with comedy was more complicated, although the genres were formally less similar.[25] Both comedy and satyr drama shared a number of characters, titles, and plots, and on occasion comic poets even used a chorus of satyrs in their plays.[26] In addition, characters in comedy, much like the chorus of satyrs, wore a phallus attached to their costume, although the comic phallus was much larger.[27] Satyrs also employ comical language of comedy's lower register (though, again comedy was much more egregious in this regard), making use of 'colloquialisms, non-verbal sounds, word play, and sexual innuendo, as well as references to food, breasts, buttocks, penises, farting, crotch-grabbing, erections, chamber pots, and other items and acts not found in tragedy'.[28]

The earliest and most influential extant discussion of satyr play, found in Demetrius' second- or third-century *De Elocutione*, perfectly captures the genre's 'comic' and 'tragic' elements:[29]

ἔνθα μὲν γὰρ γέλωτός τε χρεία καὶ χαρίτων, ἐν σατύρῳ καὶ ἐν κωμῳδίαις, τραγῳδία δὲ χάριτας μὲν παραλαμβάνει ἐν πολλοῖς,

ὁ δὲ γέλως ἐχθρὸς τραγῳδίας· οὐδὲ γὰρ ἐπινοήσειεν ἄν τις
τραγῳδίαν παίζουσαν, ἐπεὶ σάτυρον γράψει ἀντὶ τραγῳδίας.

Demetrius, De Elocutione 168–9

> For in some [arts] there is need of both laughter and charm, as in satyr
> drama and comedy; tragedy invites charm in many instances, but
> laughter is tragedy's enemy. No one would consider [writing] a playful
> tragedy, since he would be writing a satyr play instead of a tragedy.

Demetrius' phrase 'playful tragedy' (*tragôidia paizousa*) is often used
as a descriptive catch phrase for satyr drama.[30] With so few ancient
descriptions of the genre, it provides a helpful point of reference, as
it demonstrates satyr drama's generic similarity to tragedy, while also
expressing the playful elements imparted by the chorus of satyrs.
However, as with all essentializations, the phrase fails to describe the
nuances of the genre. In fact, it even fails to describe the nuances of
Demetrius' larger discussion, which clearly depicts satyr drama as a
genre separate from and in between tragedy and comedy.[31] Demetrius
repeatedly draws connections between comedy and satyr drama
because of their similar use of charm and laughter. He even notes that
comedy and satyr drama have similar 'purpose' (168), 'effects' (168),
and 'topic/context' (169). Like satyrs, who look part human and part
animal but transcend both categories, satyr drama looks part tragedy
and part comedy, but transcends both categories.

History of satyr drama

The origins of satyr drama are unknown, but the genre was presumably
shaped by a variety of archaic performance types, some of which may
not even have included satyrs.[32] The genre's primary models, though,
would most likely have been the various satyric performances
depicted on archaic vases from Athens and the Argolid. Particularly
suggestive are several Attic representations of satyrs in procession.

For example, an Athenian cup from around the middle of the sixth century portrays a group of men carrying a giant satyr on top of an oversized phallus pole (Figure 1.3). An Attic skyphos from the late sixth century similarly focuses on the procession, with a costumed satyr sitting opposite Dionysus as both figures are pulled through the city on a wheeled cart shaped like a ship (Figure 1.4). These Athenian parades obviously differ from a full-fledged theatrical production, but they are public performances connected to Dionysus and the phallophoria, and as such would have helped shape the portrayal of satyrs in the earliest period of satyr drama.

There is little in the way of definite literary evidence from the initial years of satyr play, but the explosion of satyr vases around the end of the sixth century and start of the fifth century suggests that Athenians officially instituted the genre at the City Dionysia around this time.[33] The earliest extant example of a vase to depict a classical-style satyr costume is a potsherd from around 490–470 by the Eucharides Painter

Figure 1.3 Oversized satyr riding phallus Pole (Side B), Attic black-figure lip-cup, unattributed. Florence 3897: Soprintendenza alle Antichità.

Figure 1.4 Dionysus and satyr in a wheeled ship cart, Attic black-figure skyphos, *c.* 530–500, Theseus Painter. Acr 1281a, National Archaeological Museum, Athens. © Hellenic Ministry of Education and Religious Affairs, Culture and Sports.

(Figure 1.5). There are, however, a number of vases from earlier dates that are suggestive of satyr play.[34] The oldest of these is a late sixth-century Attic red-figure volute crater (Figure 1.6), on which a group of satyrs attempts to steal Heracles' weapons while the hero sleeps.[35] The satyrs have no particular markers of costume, but the musician playing the *aulos* on the far left suggests that it is, if not a satyr play, a satyric performance depicting a mythological scene in the manner of a satyr play.[36]

The production period of these satyr vases corresponds to a notice found in the tenth-century CE Byzantine encyclopaedia known as the *Suda*, which states that the first satyr dramatist was Pratinas of Phlius. Although his date of birth is unknown, he apparently competed against Aeschylus in 499 and had passed away by 467, dates that place

Figure 1.5 Attic red-figure amphora fragment, *c.* 490–470, Eucharides Painter, The J. Paul Getty Museum, Villa Collection, Malibu, California. 86. AE.190.6. Terracotta.

Figure 1.6 Satyrs robbing the sleeping Heracles, Attic red-figure volute crater, *c.* 510. Padula, Museo Archaeologico Provinciale della Lucania Occidentale.

him in the early years of the festival.[37] Nevertheless, the language found in the *Suda* remains problematic. Even if Pratinas was, indeed, the 'first to write satyr plays', this record probably refers only to satyr plays in Athens, not the rest of Greece. In fact, he may have brought satyr drama from his home in the Argolid. A few of Pratinas' titles are extant (*Dymaenae* or *Caryatids, Perseus, Tantalus, Satyr Wrestlers*), as are a few fragments,[38] but none of his poetic remains can be linked to satyr drama with complete certainty. The longest extant fragment (the 'hyporcheme', *TrGF* 1² F3), however, is sung by a group of satyrs and can, thus, be connected to satyr drama with a fair amount of certainty, even though its style and content differ from later satyr plays like Euripides' *Cyclops*.

In Pratinas' hyporcheme, as Athenaeus (14.617b) dubs it, the satyr chorus appears to be annoyed at current trends in the theatre, particularly the growing prominence of the *aulos* (a recorder-like musical instrument) in choral performances.[39] The satyrs sing:

What is this noise? What are these dances?
    What is this outrage at the tumultuous
    altar of Dionysus?
Bromius is mine, mine.
    It is my role to sing loudly; it is for me to make noise,
    dancing along the mountains with the Naiads,
just like a swan leading
its dappled-wing melody.
The Pierian Muse has determined the queenly
song: let the *aulos*
dance the second part.
For it is the servant.
It can only lead the revel
and the brawls of drunk young
men fighting in doorways.
Strike the one who has
the voice of a spotted toad.
Burn the spit-wasting reed,
that babbling, off-beat, out of tune
tool shaped by a drill.
Look at me, flinging my hands and feet.

Thriambodithyrambus, ivy-crowned lord,
listen, listen to my Dorian dance.

This fragment – if it does in fact come from a satyr play – provides a remarkable window into the earliest period of satyr drama. The satyrs break dramatic illusion, sing in an overtly melic style, and abuse the *aulos* and, by association, the *aulos* player. One of the most noteworthy elements of the fragment is the satyrs' obsession with Dionysus and the Dionysiac. They sing of the god's altar, claiming that Bromius (i.e. Dionysus) is theirs, and the fragment ends with a self-aware, meta-performative reference to the chorus' own actions, the flinging hands and feet of their dance, as they directly address the 'ivy-crowned lord'.

As Pratinas' fragment demonstrates, Dionysus appears to have played a crucial role in satyr drama's early development, and playwrights continued to highlight the genre's Dionysian connections in their satyr plays throughout the fifth century.[40] Dionysus appeared onstage as a character in a number of satyric productions. In Sophocles' *Dionysiskos*, Silenus and the satyrs care for the god when he is a baby, and in Aeschylus' *Theoroi* or *Isthmiastae*, Dionysus bursts onstage to complain that the satyrs have abandoned their religious duties to become athletes.[41] Even when Dionysus is not a character, other figures in the play frequently mention him or sing his praises.[42] For example, in Sophocles' *Ichneutae*, a satyr play for which we have approximately four hundred verses, the myth itself centres on Apollo and Hermes, but as soon as the nymph Cyllene sees the chorus, she mentions the god.[43] She wonders (224) why the satyrs are bothering her and not taking part in their traditional Dionysiac revelries. Sophocles uses the presence of the satyrs and the absence of Dionysus to incorporate the god into a myth in which he previously had no role.

As far as we can tell, satyr dramatists of the fifth century exclusively used mythological plots, but certain myths were more appropriate than others.[44] Tragedians writing satyr plays avoided stories that would be found in tragedies, focusing instead on myths with happy conclusions. For example, in his trilogy of tragedies known as the *Oresteia*, Aeschylus tells the story of Agamemnon's murder at the hands of his wife Clytemnestra (*Agamemnon*), their son Orestes' revenge-murder of Aegisthus and Clytemnestra (*Libation Bearers*), and the complicated divine intervention needed to end the cycle of retributive justice (*Eumenides*). The satyr play that followed these tragedies, however, the *Proteus* (*TrGF* 3 F210-215), staged the story of Agamemnon's brother Menelaus, who was shipwrecked in Egypt on his way home after the Trojan War.[45] Despite the calamitous-sounding plot, the play takes a favourable turn, with the hero catching the shape-shifting sea divinity Proteus and learning how he and his men, along with the satyrs, can return to Greece. Dramatists focused their satyr plays on particular plots that led to favourable conclusions, such as the defeat of monstrous ogres and villains, the discovery of new inventions, the care of divine or heroic infants, and the appearance of characters from the underworld.

Most of what we know about satyr drama's development comes from the fifth century, but the genre also has an interesting and complex history after the death of the 'great three' tragedians.[46] Sometime around the middle of the fourth century, satyr drama was removed from its traditional place at the conclusion of a tragedian's competitive entry. In fact, it was removed from competition altogether. Didascalic records indicate that only one play was staged each year at the start of the festival,[47] and although our knowledge of the genre is extremely fragmentary during the late Classical and early Hellenistic periods, a faint image of a more experimental satyr drama emerges. Chaeremon's *Centaur* (*TrGF* 1² F9a-11), for example, appears to have been a satyr play with such remarkable metrical playfulness that Aristotle calls it 'a mixed recitation of all meters'.[48] Astydamas the Younger also plays with certain generic expectations, when he alludes to his performance's own performance, breaking dramatic illusion by discussing the obligations of a playwright in a meta-poetic, gastronomic metaphor:

ἀλλ' ὥσπερ δείπνου γλαφυροῦ ποικίλην εὐωχίαν
τὸν ποιητὴν δεῖ παρέχειν τοῖς θεαταῖς τὸν σοφόν,
ἵν' ἀπίῃ τις τοῦτο φαγὼν καὶ πιών, ὅπερ λαβὼν
χαίρει <τις>, καὶ σκευασία μὴ μί' ᾖ τῆς μουσικῆς

TrGF 1² F4

A clever poet should supply his audience with
a rich feast that resembles an elegant dinner,
so everyone eats and drinks whatever he likes before
he leaves, and the entertainment doesn't consist of a single course.

Trans. Olson 2008

Such a discussion of the art of poetry appears to have been uncharacteristic of the mythological productions of fifth-century satyr drama and, in rupturing theatrical illusion, was much more characteristic of fifth-century comedy.[49]

Another way in which the remains of late fourth- and early third-century satyr plays appear more traditionally 'comic' than satyric is in the use of *onomasti komôidein*, the abuse of contemporary figures by name.[50] The third-century Alexandrian playwright Lycophron of Chalcis (*TrGF* 1² F2-3) attacks the philosopher Menedemus for his stinginess and unrestrained moralizing, and during the same period, Sositheus of Alexandria Troas (*TrGF* 1² F4) ridicules the philosopher Cleanthes of Assus for repelling students of stoicism with his stupidity. The most famous example of satiric satyr play comes from Python of Catania's *Agen* (*TrGF* 1² F1), a 'little satyr play' (*satyrikon dramation*, Athenaeus *Deipnosophistae* 13.586d and 595e) that abuses Alexander the Great's disloyal satrap, Harpalus.[51] Not only did Harpalus pilfer money to support his exorbitant lifestyle in Babylon, but he also spent massive amounts of Alexander's wealth venerating the courtesans Pythionice and Glycera (the topic of the play's opening scene).

After this experimental stage of satyr play, the genre went through periods of growth and decline, but no literary remains have survived from the second century onward. Inscriptional records reveal moments at which 'old', re-performed satyr plays held a central a position in the festival; other times, they show that new satyr plays were performed outside Athens at different religious festivals.[52] Satyr drama even survived into the Roman Republic and Empire.[53] Ultimately, our understanding of satyr drama at any given period is extremely fragmented, and any conclusions that we draw must remain speculative. Nevertheless, from the sixth century's mysterious satyric processions to the third century's abusively 'comic' productions, the fragmentary remains of satyr play reveal enough pieces of an intricate puzzle that we are able to sense the complexity of trends and transformations in satyr drama's development.

Functions of the genre

Like the history of satyr drama, the functions of the genre are uncertain and open to debate. It is unlikely that a modern reader can fully grasp the depth and variety of meanings that satyr drama held for the original Athenian audience, but scholars have conjectured a number of reasonable functions.[54] Some have seen satyr drama as a pleasant and humorous way to ease the mind after the psychological demands of tragedy, or as a parody of the preceding tragic performances. Others believe that satyr plays represented certain Athenian male fantasies or offered a means of exploring the 'other', or that they served as a negative educational paradigm. One of the most influential recent theories is that satyr drama reasserted a collective male Athenian consciousness after the 'feminine' experience of tragedy.[55] Satyr drama lent itself to a range of civic, social, and psychological functions, but its most important role was in its religious connection to Dionysus.[56]

To understand satyr drama's Dionysian function at the god's festival, it is necessary to examine the historical and legendary accounts of satyr drama's introduction to the Athenian festival. As with most discussions on the history of the theatre, Aristotle's *Poetics* presents the launching point:

ἐκ μικρῶν μύθων καὶ λέξεως γελοίας διὰ τὸ ἐκ
σατυρικοῦ μεταβαλεῖν ὀψὲ ἀπεσεμνύνθη.

Aristotle, *Poetics* 1449a, 18–20

After a period of slight plots and laughable speech, owing to development from a satyric ethos, it was at a late stage that tragedy acquired dignity.

Trans. Halliwell, in Halliwell et al., 1995

Although Aristotle wrote two centuries after the organization of the City Dionysia and his comments are challenging to unravel, there are two points that deserve attention here.[57] First, Aristotle uses the adjective *satyrikon*, rather than the traditional technical terms *satyroi* or *satyrikon drama*, which suggests that he may be differentiating satyr drama from some pre-tragic, pre-satyr-drama performance that was 'satyr-drama like' or had a 'satyric ethos'.[58] This is key to the second point, which is that satyr drama did not predate tragedy in any official way.[59] Tragedy was instituted before the official introduction of satyr drama, and during the earliest period, audiences probably had far fewer expectations for the genre. Modern audiences have a distinct sense of the tragic, but this was much less the case for ancient Athenians. Plots were quite diverse, especially in the late sixth and early fifth centuries, and they developed over time to create the serious genre we now associate with the term.[60] With these qualifications in mind, we can see that Aristotle may have been suggesting that tragedy grew out of a sort of less-developed, less-dignified performance that contained the 'slight plots and laughable speech' one would associate with satyr plays of his time.

Whether or not Aristotle is correct that satyric performances developed into tragedy, satyr drama as an official genre came after tragedy, and it appears to have been instituted for a particular religious function. According to ancient legend, the City Dionysia was established in honour of the god Dionysus, and the plots of the earliest tragedies reflected this connection.[61] However, tragedians shifted the content of their productions and began depicting stories not directly related to the god's mythological history. This led some spectators to object that drama had improperly evolved to have 'Nothing to do with Dionysus'. The *Suda* explains:

> τὸ πρόσθεν εἰς τὸν Διόνυσον γράφοντες τούτοις ἠγωνίζοντο, ἅπερ καὶ σατυρικὰ ἐλέγετο· ὕστερον δὲ μεταβάντες εἰς τὸ τραγῳδίας γράφειν κατὰ μικρὸν εἰς μύθους καὶ ἱστορίας ἐτράπησαν, μηκέτι τοῦ Διονύσου μνημονεύοντες· ὅθεν τοῦτο καὶ ἐπεφώνησαν.
>
> Suda O 806

> Previously, when writing for Dionysus, they competed with these works, which were called 'satyric'. But later, having switched to the writing of tragedies, they turned little by little to myths and historical subjects, no longer being mindful of Dionysus. Because of this, they shouted this phrase ['Nothing to do with Dionysus'].

Although the *Suda* offers no source for the history provided here, the account corresponds to Aristotle's report that during the sixth century tragedy grew from something satyric into a more complex genre.[62] More importantly, however, it suggests that tragedy evolved away from Dionysian narratives, which prompted opposition from the audience.

Satyr drama, it seems, was instituted to re-establish Dionysiac themes at the god's festival. As we saw in the previous section, a number of authors explicitly incorporate the god into the plots of their satyr plays, while others incorporate him by drawing attention to his absence. This is especially true of Euripides' *Cyclops*, where Silenus, the satyrs, and Polyphemus constantly refer to Dionysus' absence from the island. In addition to these direct references to the god, the satyrs themselves naturally lend a Dionysian quality to satyr plays, since they love Bacchic wine, song, and dance, and they regularly take part in Dionysian dress-up, assuming the role of athletes, fishermen, or nurses.[63] Dionysus is also featured through the religious message implicit in most satyr plays. The satyrs are always rescued and restored to their previous happy life with Dionysus, a plotline that reflects the god's religious role in ancient Greece: he offers safety and a second life separate from the troubles one faces in this world.[64] By placing satyr plays at the end of the tetralogy, after three tragedies, the Athenians gave satyr drama a certain pride of place. Not only was it the last play staged before judging, but it capped the entire day's theatrical experience and reincorporated Dionysiac elements into the festival after a trilogy of tragedies that (often) had 'Nothing to do with Dionysus'.

The mythological background: Homer's *Odyssey*

As we move from satyr drama generally to Euripides' *Cyclops* specifically, the most obvious entry point is the mythological plot on which the play is based. Unlike most surviving Greek tragedies, the precise literary model for Euripides' *Cyclops* is extant, and to understand the play as the author and his audience understood it, we must examine the original in detail. The mythological prototype for the *Cyclops* is Homer's *Odyssey*, the focus of which is Odysseus' ten-year-long journey back home to the island of Ithaca after ten years fighting in the Trojan War. Homer intertwines events from the lives of Odysseus' son Telemachus and his wife Penelope, the queen of Ithaca, and relates the various challenges these characters face, but the primary narrative centres on the hero himself. The most famous section of the *Odyssey* is, undoubtedly, Odysseus' personal account of the physical, emotional, and psychological challenges that he faced on his journey homeward (books nine through twelve). Within this narrative, Odysseus' contact with Polyphemus in book nine is not only the most celebrated story, but it also presents the original version of the myth that Euripides adapted for his satyric *Cyclops*.[65]

Prior to Odysseus' narrative in book nine, Odysseus has spent seven years trapped on the island of Ogygia. The messenger-god Hermes, though, persuades Calypso to free the hero so he may continue his journey home. After Odysseus builds a raft and sets off, the sea-god Poseidon stirs up a treacherous storm and wrecks the boat, but the sea nymph Ino comes to Odysseus' aid. He reaches the island of the Phaeacians, and the following morning, the young princess Nausicaa finds him naked by the shore and urges him to entreat her parents, Alcinous and Arete, for their care. The king and queen receive the hero according to the Homeric code of guest-host relations (*xenia*) and welcome him into their home without knowing his name. Then, at a large feast hosted by Alcinous, Odysseus asks the blind poet Demodocus to recount the story of the Trojan horse, but when the hero hears the tale, he is overwhelmed with emotion, divulges his identity, and launches into his own narrative of the events that led him to the island of the Phaeacians.

Odysseus' personal account is the most central and well-known section of the epic poem. Over the course of four books, Odysseus sings of encounters with various obstacles, many of which were supernatural. The flowery food of the Lotus-eaters made his men forget about returning home. The monstrous Laestrygonians were giant cannibals who wished to devour Odysseus and his sailors. The witch Circe changed Odysseus' men into swine. The Sirens sang their enchanting and deadly song in hopes of luring Odysseus to his death. The six-headed monster Scylla snatched Odysseus' crewmates from her hiding place in the cliffs. And the giant whirlpool Charybdis nearly swallowed Odysseus on two occasions. The most famous event, however, comes in book nine, when Odysseus encounters the son of Poseidon, the one-eyed giant Polyphemus.

According to Odysseus' report, he and his men were passing by Cape Malea, a peninsula in the southeast of the Peloponnese, when the North Wind drove them off course. The wind and waves battered them for nine days, but finally they landed on a fertile, uninhabited island near the homeland of the Cyclopes. Odysseus and the crew of his twelve ships arrived at night and slept on the shore. The next morning three groups of men hunted down more than one hundred goats, and they feasted all day on meat and on wine that had been stored in their ships. When they gazed across to the nearby land of the Cyclopes, they saw smoke and heard the monsters' voices and the bleating of their sheep and goats. After another night of sleep, Odysseus gathered his men and ordered them to remain on the island, while he took his crew and his ship to 'make trial' of the Cyclopes and 'to learn who they are, whether they are cruel, and wild, and unjust, or whether they are kind to strangers and fear the gods in their thoughts'.[66]

When Odysseus and his men arrived, they found a high cave, many sheep and goats, and a high courtyard with large stones and tall trees. Polyphemus, the 'monstrous marvel' (9.190), lived here and shepherded his flocks, alone and away from all the other Cyclopes. Odysseus chose twelve companions to accompany him on his exploration of the area, while the rest stayed by the ship. He brought provisions and a goatskin of wine that had been given to him by Maron, the son of the wine-god. When he arrived at the cave, he found no one there, but entered anyway, finding cheeses, pens crowded with lambs, whey measured out in various containers, and numerous bowls full of fresh milk. Odysseus' comrades begged him to take some of the animals and cheeses to the ship and flee, but Odysseus' curiosity remained – he insisted on staying so that he could meet whoever lived there and see if he would give them appropriate guest-gifts.

While they waited, the Greek heroes started a fire, made a sacrifice, and helped themselves to the cheeses, but when the giant, one-eyed Polyphemus finally appeared, they were so frightened that they hid in the recesses of the cave. The Cyclops, who failed to notice the men, placed a massive stone in the doorway, milked his flock, curdled half the milk, and stored the other half. When he started a fire, he spotted Odysseus and his men, and in a monstrous voice, asked who they were, from where they had come, and what their business was. Odysseus recounted his labours in the Trojan War and established himself as a suppliant, to which Polyphemus responded by calling him a fool, telling him that the Cyclopes pay no heed to Zeus. Then the monster asked Odysseus where the hero left his ship, but Odysseus lied and told him that Poseidon had dashed it to pieces and that he and his men had barely escaped. Without a word, Polyphemus jumped up, grabbed two of Odysseus' companions, smashed them on the ground, and made them his dinner, eating everything including their bones and entrails. Polyphemus then drank some milk and fell asleep. Although Odysseus wanted to kill the giant, he realized that he and his men would never be able to remove the enormous stone from the cave's doorway.

The next morning, Polyphemus removed the rock, drove out his flocks, and replaced the stone to trap Odysseus and his men. Odysseus devised a plan to sharpen the tip of a huge olive tree that was in the cave and harden it in the fire while Polyphemus was out, so that he and his men could grind it into the eye of the giant while he was sleeping. After Polyphemus returned and ate more of the seamen, Odysseus brought him a bowl of Maron's wine. The Cyclops immediately gulped it down and asked Odysseus his name, saying he would give the Greek hero a guest gift that would make him happy. When Polyphemus had consumed three bowls and was feeling drunk, Odysseus played his famous trick, telling the Cyclops that 'Noman' or

'Nobody' (Οὖτις) was his name, to which Polyphemus responded that his guest-gift would be to eat Nobody last of all.[67]

Suddenly, Polyphemus passed out and vomited up wine and chunks of human flesh, giving Odysseus time to reheat the olive wood and hearten his men. Just as the wood was about to catch fire, a daemon breathed great courage into them, and they plunged it into the monster's eye, spinning it like a drill. His eyelids were scorched and his eyeball crackled and hissed, and Odysseus and his men hid behind the rocks, while Polyphemus shouted in pain to his fellow Cyclopes. When the neighbouring monsters came to the cave, Polyphemus shouted through the stone barrier 'My friends, it is Nobody that is slaying me by guile and not by force',[68] which prompted the other Cyclopes to leave him alone, misinterpreting 'Nobody' for 'nobody'. In an attempt to catch Odysseus and his men, Polyphemus groped his way to the door, removed the rock, and sat down with his arms outstretched, but Odysseus tied three sheep together and placed one man under each middle animal so they could escape unnoticed. When dawn broke, the flocks and crew went out, and Odysseus himself escaped by holding onto the belly of the finest ram.

As Odysseus passed the threshold of the cave, Polyphemus addressed his favourite ram in a charming speech that imagines the animal to be saddened by the Cyclops' woes. The monster sent the animal on its way, and Odysseus escaped, untied his men, drove the sheep to the ship, and they all sailed off together. Being angry and reckless, though, Odysseus mockingly shouted from the sea that Zeus had taken vengeance on the monster for not honouring the laws of *xenia* (the guest-host relationship).[69] This gave Polyphemus a sense of where Odysseus' ship was, so he broke off a chunk of the mountain and threw it into the sea, forcing the boat back to shore. As the men rowed away a second time, they begged Odysseus to stay quiet, but they could not stop him from revealing his identity to the Cyclops. Polyphemus immediately recalled a prophecy he had once received that a man named Odysseus would blind him, but he never suspected it would be a man of such small stature. He then prayed to his father Poseidon that Odysseus never reach his homeland or, if it is fated for him to return, that he arrive late, suffering, without his comrades, and in someone else's ship. The Cyclops threw one last massive stone, which landed just behind the boat and propelled it onward to safety.

The date and text of the *Cyclops*

With a broad understanding of satyrs, satyr drama, and the play's Homeric model, we can move on to examine the *Cyclops* as a performance (Chapter 2), but first it is important to survey the history of the text as it has been passed down to us. The precise performance date of Euripides' *Cyclops* has not been transmitted from antiquity and is, ultimately, impossible to know with certainty. However, numerous scholars have attempted to date the play based on historical, literary, metrical, thematic, and stylistic criteria.[70] Earlier scholars believed that the *Cyclops* was one of Euripides' oldest plays, but Richard Seaford, who dates the play to 408, and Matthew Wright, who dates the play to 412, offer the most convincing and comprehensive arguments.[71] As they point out, the *Cyclops* exhibits certain metrical similarities to Euripides' late plays, the *Helen* (412) and *Phoenissae* (409), and there appear to be certain intertexts with Aristophanes' *Thesmophoriazusae* (411) and Sophocles' *Philoctetes* (409). The *Cyclops* also seems to have particular thematic connections to Euripides' *Helen*, *Andromeda*, and *Iphigenia among the Taurians*, tragedies that Wright links to the City Dionysia of 412. The location of the *Cyclops* in Sicily may also connect the play to Athens' Sicilian expedition of 413, in which the Athenians faced one of their greatest defeats of the Peloponnesian War. These various strands of evidence suggest that Euripides most likely staged his satyr play at some point between 412 and 408.

The history of Euripides' *Cyclops* after its original performance is also uncertain. The textual tradition suggests that it was preserved not because of its majesty or because ancient scholars considered it an essential play or a perfect example of the genre.[72] Satyr plays did not receive much scholarly attention in antiquity, and they were not used as educational texts. The fact that we lack so many satyr plays suggests that they were not even recorded with the same vigour as tragedy. Simply put, the *Cyclops* is extant because of a fortunate turn of events. While the seven surviving plays of Aeschylus and the seven extant plays of Sophocles were clearly selected for transmission because of their content, their grandeur, and their timelessness, only ten of Euripides' nineteen extant plays were preserved in the primary medieval tradition. The other nine plays were assembled in a manuscript (and its offshoots) merely because of their names. The Laurentian text (named after the library in Florence that houses the manuscript, and abbreviated as 'L') contains these nine plays in alphabetical order from epsilon to kappa: *Helen, Electra, Children of Heracles, Heracles, Suppliant Women, Iphigenia in Aulis, Iphigenia among the Taurians, Ion, and Cyclops.* We are, of course, fortunate to have this entire volume, but the fact that the *Cyclops* is the last play in the collection is a particularly extraordinary stroke of luck.

Manuscript L was penned around 1320 by the Byzantine intellectual Demetrius Triclinius, a scholar famed for his careful editing and analysis of ancient Greek texts, especially theatrical texts. The manuscript indicates that after the first copy was made, Demetrius revised it by comparing it to the exemplar. He then later added textual corrections and emendations in two further attempts to edit the plays. For years, Manuscript L was considered inferior to Manuscript P (housed in the Vatican Library Palatinus in Rome), but Zuntz has shown that P was actually copied from L after Demetrius' first edits but before the second and third set of corrections.[73] Manuscript P, then, offers little help in attaining the 'correct' text of the *Cyclops*, but it is occasionally valuable for revealing original readings that Triclinius altered in L, or for offering speculations by later authors who added to the manuscript. The situation is similar with two other copies of L that were written in Italy around 1500, since they provide a few important corrections and conjectures.[74]

The only remains of the *Cyclops* that predate L are quotes preserved in the works of other ancient authors and one papyrus fragment from the fourth century CE.[75] Both of these sources offer occasional divergences from L, none of which are particularly important in their substance, but are nonetheless useful, since they demonstrate the inherent problems and uncertainties with contemporary 'authoritative' texts, and they help explain some of the textual issues that still impede interpretation of the *Cyclops*. For example, the late second-century/ early third-century CE author of the *Deipnosophistae*, Athenaeus (1.36d), quotes verse 534 as:

πλήγας ὁ κῶμος λοίδορόν θ᾽ ὕβριν φέρει
The revel brings blows and abusive violence.

Manuscript L, however, offers:

πυγμὰς ὁ κῶμος λοίδορόν τ᾽ ἔριν φιλεῖ
The revel brings fists and abusive strife.

The sense of these verses is close enough that choosing between them is of little consequence to the play's meaning. One could even make the argument that because Athenaeus wrote around the end of the third century CE that his text should take precedence over L (it is nearly a millennium older than L), but another verse quoted in the *Deipnosophistae* illustrates the problem with this argument. In citing verse 136 of the *Cyclops*, Athenaeus (14.658c) writes:

καὶ τυρὸς ὀπίας ἔστι καὶ Διὸς γάλα.
There is curdled cheese and Zeus' milk.

L, however, says:

καὶ τυρὸς ὀπίας ἔστι καὶ βοὸς γάλα.
There is curdled cheese and cow's milk.

The reading in Athenaeus' *Deipnosophistae* obviously makes no sense, and L presents, if not the original text, something much closer to Euripides' original.

As this example makes clear, when reading an ancient text, we must remember how inexact the transmission process was before the printing press, especially if that text – like the *Cyclops* – comes down to us in only one textual tradition. Ancient scribes, scholars, and slaves who recorded texts inevitably introduced errors into their transcriptions.[76] Many of these were simple mistakes common to any act of copying, but the lack of many orthographic conventions that we take for granted also made copying problematic. For example, when Euripides wrote his *Cyclops*, it was not common to use spaces between words or punctuation within lines, nor were there any stage directions or marks to indicate a change in speaker. The most serious problem in the transmission of a theatrical text like Euripides' *Cyclops* was that actors regularly altered texts and interpolated lines when travelling troupes copied scripts for re-performance. This became such an issue for the Greeks that within a century of Euripides' death, the Athenian statesman Lycurgus recommended a law that the plays of Aeschylus, Sophocles, and Euripides be preserved and cross-checked with actors' scripts before plays were staged.[77] Although the Athenians passed this law, actors continued to modify texts until scholars at the Alexandrian library compiled standard editions around 200.[78] During the many centuries that followed, textual errors persisted to creep in even to these official texts, and Euripides' *Cyclops* remains the sole surviving satyr play to attest to this imperfect tradition of textual transmission.

2

Viewing the Play: Plot and Performance

When we sit down to read ancient Greek drama, it is easy to forget that plays were not intended to be read, but to be staged. Aeschylus, Sophocles, Euripides, and Aristophanes were the *didaskaloi* ('teachers' or 'directors') for their own plays, which means they instructed the actors and choruses on their blocking, gestures, intonation, choreography, even the notes of their songs. Because playwrights oversaw nearly every element of their productions as they prepared their cast and crew for a single performance, ancient texts do not include stage directions, a fact that complicates interpretation for modern audiences.[1] Our goal as readers should be, as much as possible, to use literary and artistic evidence to envision the play as it was originally staged. This chapter will provide a thorough study of the *Cyclops'* plot and performance, walking the reader through the original viewing experience. We will examine the technical components of each scene and will analyse dialogues, hymns, and speeches in order to work out the action of the play, from the initial entrance of Silenus to the triumphal exit of Odysseus and the satyrs. Close readings of fragmentary satyr plays and ancient satyr vases will help supply information about the *Cyclops'* costumes, masks, props, dances, and other matters of dramaturgy.

Setting the scene

In *De Architectura*, Vitruvius describes satyr drama's physical backdrop as 'trees, caves, mountains, and the rest of those rustic items that give the look of a decorated landscape'.[2] Vitruvius, however, was writing at the beginning of the first century CE, and we have only a limited sense of what scenery was like during Euripides' time. The term *skênê*, from which 'scenery' is derived, was the Greek word for tent, and in the first years of the theatre it probably referred to a tent or tent-like structure that functioned as an entrance and exit point for actors.[3] By the time Euripides staged the *Cyclops*, technical arts and theatrical narratives had become more involved, which suggests that artists used improved perspective, illusion, and realism in scenery. Nevertheless, the *skênê* was probably a simple, removable wooden backdrop or painted curtain that signified Polyphemus' cave (complete with exit to the area backstage). There may also have been *paraskênia*, which were wings on both sides of the *skênê* that displayed scenic painting. In the *Cyclops*, these would perhaps have depicted the sea on one side and rocks or pastures on the other. By 420, the stage had also been elevated to about one metre above the orchestra.[4] In the *Cyclops*, this stage functioned as the central point of action, although the chorus occupied the orchestra space in front of the stage.

Euripides may also have used the natural outdoor location of the theatre to help set the scene. The theatre of Dionysus was built on the southern hill of the Acropolis, and the sprawling, sunlit, natural surroundings could easily have been incorporated into the *Cyclops'* setting near Mt. Aetna in Sicily. In fact, the natural backdrop probably reduced the impact of the manufactured set significantly, which suggests that the painted scenery may have worked in a purely pragmatic, general way. If Euripides did include specific painted details on his *skênê*, the majority of the audience may not have been able to see them, since the theatre seated thousands of people, many of whom were far from the stage.[5] The various constraints of ancient scenography most likely led to a simple backdrop that would have placed the onus on the audience to imagine certain components of the scenery, while ignoring other features that hindered the illusion of being in Sicily (e.g. Pericles' Odeion, which was just to the west of the theatre). At the start of the play, the audience, who had just finished watching three of Euripides' tragedies, was presented with new scenery. It is possible, even likely, that the audience had seen the *Cyclops*' backdrop (or something very similar) before, since satyr drama was so frequently set in rural locations. Verse 47 indicates that there was a water trough near the cave entrance for the flocks, but again the audience may have been expected to envision this simple prop, since it does not play any particular role in the remainder of the production.

Prologue (1–40)

The action of the play begins with the entrance of Silenus, the elderly father of the satyrs. If the Pronomos Vase (Figure 2.1) gives an accurate sense of costume, Silenus was a surprisingly dignified-looking figure.[6] The actor wore a body stocking with white tufts to indicate the satyr's advanced years, and the mask was detailed, with long white hair and beard, a wrinkled forehead, and perhaps a wreath of ivy. He had a horse's tail attached in the back and a phallus attached to the front. The vase clearly depicts Silenus' costume phallus as small and unobtrusive, in the tradition of decorous Athenians (and *not* in the tradition of indecorous archaic satyrs[7]), but the language in the play itself suggests that Silenus' phallus in the *Cyclops* played too important a role visually to be so small.[8]

When Silenus walks onstage from the cave, he holds a rake (one of very few props in the play[9]), and the first words he utters are a direct address to the god Dionysus (ὦ Βρόμιε, v. 1). There is a slight ironic playfulness in this address, since the chorus and actors repeatedly note that the god is absent from the island where they are stranded, but in the theatre at the performance, Dionysus was actually present in the form of a statue.[10] Silenus immediately begins lamenting the labours

Figure 2.1 Pronomos Vase, Attic red-figure krater, *c.* 410, Pronomos Painter. Naples, Museo Nazionale 81673.

that he has been forced to endure on behalf of the god, both as a young man and now in his old age. He uses the same word that is used of great heroes' labours (πόνους), which suggests that, to his mind, he has taken part in dangerous missions on par with the greatest of the Greeks, both mythological and historical. He lists various adventures with the god, including Hera's infliction of madness on Dionysus and the Olympian deities' battle with the earth-born giants in the Gigantomachy. His language indicates that he probably mimicked these labours throughout the scene, grabbing his make-believe shield and striking the giant Enceladus with his imagined sword. Despite the heroic stylings, the audience would have known that these activities were not typical of the cowardly Silenus. Even Silenus himself stops mid-stab to ask, 'Wait, did I dream all this' (v. 8)? But he resumes his bravado, doubling down on his bravery in a manner that establishes Euripides' Silenus in his traditional role: a bombastic liar who even believes his own lies.

The culmination of Silenus' complaints serves to clarify the events that have led to his current predicament, which is the worst he has ever experienced. The goddess Hera inspired the Tyrrhenian pirates to kidnap Dionysus, and he and his satyr-children embarked on a journey to rescue the god.[11] When they were negotiating the seas near Cape Malea, however, they were blown off course and shipwrecked on Sicily, where the one-eyed children of Poseidon—the Cyclopes—live their uncivilized lives. One Cyclops in particular, Polyphemus, caught and enslaved the entire troupe of satyrs, forcing Silenus to take care of the cave and prepare meals, while his children care for the flocks, a stark contrast to the Bacchic revelries they would typically enjoy. Throughout the entire monologue/prologue, Silenus uses a particular mode of storytelling that signals a good deal of humorous mimicry. Of particular note is the way in which he dynamically describes taking his stand at the stern of the boat and steering the ship, while his sons grabbed their oars and rowed. The mention of his young 'flesh' (δέμας, v. 2), combined with his recurring use of the term δόρυ ('spear' and 'rudder') at the end of three lines suggests that he may have been holding his costume phallus throughout this scene as he imitated stabbing and steering a ship.[12]

As the prologue comes to a close, Silenus reveals that his sons, the chorus of satyrs, are out shepherding Polyphemus' flocks, while he is left to the domestic work of sweeping and preparing food. Silenus spots the satyrs returning homeward with the Cyclops' animals, and contrasts the actions he expects to see with the satyrs' actual activities. Silenus has just complained that Polyphemus forces the satyrs to look after his animals rather than take part in Dionysian revelries, but as the chorus enters, Silenus points out the swaggering dance, the rhythm, and the revel which the satyrs appear to be enjoying. The language that Silenus uses here is significant, since he paints a vivid picture of the stage action and, more importantly, because he employs formal religious and theatrical language.[13] The term *kômos* ('revel') is a ritualized word associated with drunken celebration and was a sanctioned element of the City Dionysia, and the term *sikinnis* is the official name of the satyric dance.[14] There is some debate on the specifics of the dance, but the general consensus is that it involved leaping into the air while, in turn, lifting the right arm and leg and then the left arm and leg.[15] For members of the audience, the prologue would have mixed the reverent and the irreverent in a manner that sets the tone for the remainder of the play. Silenus presents a mix of braggadocio, cheekiness, phallic wordplay (and phallic gestures), mythological 'history', religion and ritual, and meta-performative language.

Parodos (41–82)

The entrance of the chorus of satyrs in Euripides' *Cyclops*, like all satyr plays, must have been a fantastic spectacle. Ancient visual evidence indicates that the choral actors were shirtless and shoeless, but they wore furry shorts with a smallish, erect phallus attached to the front and a horse tail attached to the back. The mask, which fit over the actor's entire head, probably had dark hair and a shaggy black beard, and pointed ears. And as various vases suggest, as soon as the satyric actor put on this mask, he invariably took on the persona of the satyr. On both the Pronomos Vase (Figure 2.1) and an Apulian bell krater attributed to the Tarporley Painter (Figure 2.2), the artists depict

Figure 2.2 Three satyr choreuts, Apulian bell krater, 410–380 BCE. Attributed to the Tarporley Painter. Nicholson Museum, Sydney, Australia, NM 47.05. Courtesy: The Nicholson Museum.

young men holding satyr masks. The sole choreut who wears his mask on each vase is distinguished from the others by his dancing. Once a member of the chorus puts on a mask, he takes on the satyric persona that the mask represents. In fact, the masked choreut on the Pronomos Vase throws his arms and legs in the air in a visual representation of the *sikinnis*; he also faces his body towards the viewer in a vulgar manner that is befitting of comic figures, but considered inappropriate for citizens.[16] Silenus describes the satyrs' dancing as lively, rhythmic, revelrous, and 'swaggering'.[17]

Beyond the raucous, rhythmic, and playfully obscene dancing of the satyrs during their entrance, it is difficult to know the precise stage action of the satyric parodos. When the chorus enters from the side-stage, which is supposed to indicate the rocky, pastoral landscape of Sicily, their first words are to the rams and ewes who fail to be corralled into their pens. The satyrs threaten to throw stones at the animals if they will not enter the cave and be locked up for the night with their young. Although this scene clearly presents interaction with various animals, it is unclear whether any sheep were actually represented onstage. It would not have been impossible to bring a small domesticated flock before an audience, or even to dress extras in sheep costumes, but it could be that the audience was expected to imagine the flocks, or that the satyrs were simply standing near the side entrance, shouting offstage to the animals. The satyrs then abruptly turn their attention in the final section of their entrance song from the animals to religion. They exclaim in metrical song and dance that there is no Dionysus on the island of the Cyclopes, no choruses, no Bacchic worship, no fresh drops of wine. They address the god directly, asking him where he has gone, shaking his golden hair, without his satyric companions. As with Silenus' prologue, the entire lament is playful and ironic, since the statue of the god Dionysus was situated in a place of prominence in the theatre, and since they themselves are a chorus worshipping Bacchus/Dionysus.

As the choral parodos comes to a close, the chorus of satyrs bemoans their forced servitude to Polyphemus and their deprivation from Dionysus' friendship. They call themselves slaves in exile, and complain that they are clothed in a 'wretched goat-skin cloak' (v. 80). Euripides addresses a major theme of the play, slavery and friendship, two interrelated and juxtaposed ideas throughout the production.[18] The satyrs praise and pray for slavery to their master Dionysus, while constantly grieving their slavery to Polyphemus, since Dionysiac slavery is based in friendship, while Cyclopean slavery is 'without friendship' (v. 81). This is a complex religious theme that is couched within a joke about the satyrs' clothing. Although it is possible that the satyrs actually wore goatskin cloaks to imitate and intimate their herdsman status, this comment may also be a metatheatrical joke. Satyrs were historically half-horse, half-man, but they also had associations with goats,[19] and Euripides seems to draw attention to the 'wretched' (v. 80) horse-goat costumes that the choreuts wear. Even if the chorus of satyrs wore dirty goat wraps, the metatheatrical joke remains, since the speakers are actors dressed as goatish horse-men, who are then dressed as goatherds. Euripides may even be referring to the etymology of tragedy in this comment about the satyrs' clothing, since *tragôidia* is literally a 'goat song', with *tragos* meaning 'goat' and *ôidê* meaning song.[20] Euripides presents various levels and layers of meaning in the parodos, but at its most basic visual level, the entrance of the satyrs offered an exciting, animated performance that would capture the audience's attention. The boisterous herding of flocks into the cave and the playfully religious and meta-poetic language would cue the audience in to the multifaceted production they were about to enjoy.

First episode (83–355)

The satyrs' raucous entrance song is ended by Silenus, who orders his children to be quiet and to have their 'attendants' (v. 83) drive the flocks into the cave. This is one of the most important comments in the first part of the play for visualizing the performance. It is not uncommon to use non-speaking actors in ancient drama,[21] and it seems that during the choral parodos and the first part of the first episode, a few extras corralled animals (which obviously makes a stronger case for the flocks being represented onstage somehow). They would have been dressed as satyrs—since Polyphemus would have eaten human attendants[22]—and they would have been used solely for the purpose of leading a few animals onto the stage from the *eisodos* and then through the central door that represented the cave. The addition of sheep, rams, and unnecessary satyrs would have added to the spectacle and humour of the parodos and first episode, since the orchestra space would have been brimming with activity.

After the satyrs order their attendants to 'go' (v. 84) in a single word command (a moment in the text that demonstrates the insignificance of the role of the extras), they ask their father why he looks so troubled. Silenus, peering offstage, says that he sees a Greek ship on the beach and a group of sailors approaching with empty containers for food and water. Silenus notes that the land at which the Greeks have arrived is *axenon*, 'not friendly to guests' (v. 91), as he recalls the most gruesome and elemental piece of the story, 'the man-eating jaw of the Cyclops' (vv. 92–3). These are the final words spoken before Odysseus enters with a small crew of men, who function as silent assistants to the hero. Odysseus addresses the group of satyrs as a whole, before he realizes that they are satyrs. The first word he utters is the direct address *xenoi* (v. 96), a term that means 'stranger', 'guest', and 'host' and is significant as a first utterance, since *xenia* ('the guest-host relationship') is a major theme of the play and of the Homeric original.[23] After asking about food and water, Odysseus realizes suddenly that he seems to have entered a city of Dionysus, since he sees an entire group of satyrs near the cave. His final words are a greeting to Silenus, and the satyr responds in turn by calling the stranger a *xenos*.

The repeated use of *xenos* would not have gone unnoticed by the audience. Euripides uses the natural ambiguity of the word to continue the theme of guest-host relations that he adopted from Homer, but he complicates the term in the next sixty lines (nearly 10 per cent of the play), a stichomythic dialogue between Silenus and Odysseus. Stichomythia is the theatrical technique of exchanging single lines back and forth. Traditionally it was used for fast-paced and often aggressive dialogue, with the intensity and rhythm of the exchange building a powerful and palpable sense of discord.[24] The dialogue begins with a humorous inversion of expectations of the guest-host relationship (rather than the monstrous inversion with Polyphemus), since Silenus rudely orders Odysseus to tell him his name and homeland. Odysseus uncharacteristically answers the satyr with a straightforward, honest response (v. 103): 'I am Ithacan Odysseus, lord of the land of Cephallenians.' Silenus responds with a literary joke, stating, οἶδ' ἄνδρα (I know the man, v. 104). Although the primary meaning of the phrase is clear, Euripides is playfully referring to Homer's *Odyssey* with the phrase's secondary meaning. Athenian theatre-goers would have been familiar with the first line of the *Odyssey* and would even have identified it primarily by its *incipit*, the first word or words of the poem: Ἄνδρα μοι ἔννεπε, Μοῦσα, πολύτροπον, ὃς …, 'Sing, Muse, of the man of many ways, who ….' Thus, when Silenus says that he 'knows the man', he also implies that he 'knows the *Odyssey*', since ἄνδρα (man) is the first word of the epic poem.[25]

Silenus' literary quip is immediately followed up with a purposefully insulting, and ironically non-Homeric, parentage for Odysseus. He calls the hero a clever chatterer, and notes that he is the son of Sisyphus. In traditional versions of the myth of Odysseus, including that of Homer's *Odyssey*, Laertes is the hero's father, but in alternate versions, Odysseus' mother, Anticleia, was already impregnated by the mythological scoundrel Sisyphus when Laertes and Anticleia married.[26] Upon Odysseus' reception, then, Silenus makes a joke at his guest's expense, implying that he was a bastard son. Although this comment would have provoked Odysseus' anger if presented in an epic or tragic context, Odysseus merely says, 'That's me, but don't be insulting' (v. 105). Odysseus' language here is significant because of the valences of the term *loidorei* (v. 105), a kind of abusive humour that Aristotle notes was outlawed in Athens.[27] Although Aristotle wrote nearly a century after Euripides, his suggestion that Athenians differentiated two types of humour, playful and abusive, is documented throughout the fifth century as well.[28] Odysseus suggests that Silenus' abuse is inappropriate mockery, and offers a corrective, as if to indicate that this style of joking is unsuitable. The humour of satyrs should be playful and childish without consequence and injury.

At this point in the play, the stage and orchestra area would probably have seemed crowded, but the focus would have been directed on Silenus and Odysseus as they quickly exchanged iambic verses.[29] This fast-paced back and forth functions almost like a prologue, providing basic background information useful for the remainder of the play. Odysseus explains that he has come from Troy, driven off course by a storm on his way home, and Silenus tells the hero where they have landed, at Mount Aetna in Sicily, a place with no city walls, no fortifications, and no men, only Cyclopes. Odysseus is the first to ask questions, and again Euripides couches the simple Homeric plot in language that is significant to contemporary Athenians: 'Who governs them? Or is rule in the hands of the people' (v. 119)? The first question is natural for the Homeric hero, but the second is humorous and anachronistic in its allusion to Athenian democracy.

Silenus responds to Odysseus' interrogations with a single word, 'solitaries' (v. 120), and explains with more Homeric literary wordplay that 'Nobody listens to anyone about anything.' In Greek, Silenus expresses the sentiment with a triple negative, intensifying the negativity with rhythm and power, 'ἀκούει δ᾽ οὐδὲν οὐδεὶς οὐδενός' ('Nobody listens to no-one no-way', v. 120). The response provides a particular aural satisfaction that makes Silenus into a poet-figure,[30] and he compounds this impression by referring to Homer's wordplay in the *Odyssey* and presaging the wordplay used later in the *Cyclops*. In the Homeric myth and later in the play, Odysseus tells Polyphemus that his name is Noman (*Outis*), ensuring that he can trick the Cyclops into escape. In Euripides' version, we see the ludicrous, gluttonous Silenus, providing inspiration for the trick, while also inverting it, using *oudeis*, a term that means the same thing as *Outis* but is actually closer to Odysseus' own name. Silenus beats Odysseus (and Homer) at his own game.

The next verses offer a barrage of questions by Odysseus for the satyr. He learns that there is no cultivation of land and that, just as in the *Odyssey*, the Cyclopes live on meat and dairy. Unlike Homer, however, Euripides deprives the island of wine. When Odysseus asks about 'Bromius' drink, the juice of the vine', Silenus offers an intriguing response that gets to the heart of satyrs and satyr drama, but also has important connections to the actual City Dionysia at which the play was performed. Instead of merely stating that the Cyclopes do not have wine, Silenus responds that they dwell in a land without dance (v. 124). This simple reply carries a good deal of meaning, for it suggests that dance is contingent on wine and that wine equals dance. This is a 'satyric' response—the satyrs love wine and dance, especially in conjunction with each other—but it also has significant religious and performative connections to the festival.[31] The Athenians organized the City Dionysia in the spring, around the time of year that buds begin to grow on grape vines. The choruses appear in Athens at Dionysus' festival just as life returns to the vine. Euripides juxtaposes the audience's current festival experience and the choruses they are seeing with Polyphemus' chorus-less land, which has no wine or Dionysus.

Odysseus' next questions turn to the Cyclopes' holiness when it comes to foreigners, and Silenus responds that these monsters think foreigners/strangers have the tastiest flesh. Silenus indicates that 'no man' (v. 128) has come to the island and not been devoured, again playing with Odysseus' name and the pun that will be used later in the play. Odysseus' mind immediately turns to escape, a distinctly different response from the Homeric original, in which Odysseus refuses to leave until after he has met the inhabitant. When the hero asks for bread, Silenus offers him meat, cheese, and milk, and Odysseus says that he can only pay with wine, a strong batch given to him by Dionysus' son, Maron. Silenus is excited at the prospect, especially since he raised Maron in his own arms, but is disappointed to see the small size of Odysseus' wineskin. Odysseus explains, though, that the skin (another important prop in the play) magically pours much more than anyone can drink.

The dialogue here is banal and practical, with Odysseus telling Silenus he has a cup in case the satyr wants a sample, but when Silenus smells and tastes the wine, he becomes much more 'satyric'. He begins uttering untranslatable sounds and making sexual jokes and gestures, as he and Odysseus split speaking single lines (hemistichomythia). Odysseus pours a splash of wine into the cup, and Silenus catches a whiff that results in the elderly satyr shouting *papaiax* (v. 153), a sound that expresses excitement and was probably accompanied by some sort of physical action, such as leaping into the air or dancing around. Silenus is no longer Polyphemus' weary slave, and as soon as he takes a sip, he is further revitalized to the point of exclaiming sounds of pleasure: *babai* and the extra-metrical *a a a* (vv. 156–7). In between these shouts of joy, Silenus cries that Bacchus is calling him to dance, as he performs a humorous and joyful jig around Odysseus.

When Silenus says that he can feel the wine gurgle all the way to the tips of his toes, Odysseus offers him some money in addition to the drink, but the satyr orders him merely to continue pouring. In exchange, Odysseus asks him to bring out some cheese or lambs, and Silenus finally breaks the stichomythic dialogue with a speech that is part abuse, part sermon. He says that he will pay little regard for his master, trading all the flocks of all the Cyclopes for a single cup of wine. His taste of the Dionysiac beverage has given him such ecstasy that he is happy to visualize his own death, saying he would happily leap from the cliffs of the Ionian island Leucas, 'drunk and with eyebrows drooping' (v. 167). This imagery fits with Silenus' other literary allusions, since the Leucadian cliffs were believed to be where Sappho committed suicide over the lost love of Phaon, and the archaic lyric poet Anacreon wrote '... from the white Leucadian cliffs I plunge, drunk with desire'.[32]

Silenus places himself in the tradition of lovers committing suicide, but instead of being drunk with desire, he is drunk with wine. He reinforces his poetic references by stating aphoristically that whoever drinks and is not happy is a mad man. But in typical satyric fashion, he manages simultaneously to undercut and augment his point by turning to a sexual joke, noting that getting drunk helps him get an erection. He expresses the idea through stage action, saying that the wine 'makes this thing stand up' (v. 169), while pointing to or grabbing his flaccid stage phallus. Silenus then lists some other effects of drinking wine: it helps him 'grab hold of a breast' and stroke a woman's 'bush' with his hands.[33] The satyr mixes the literal with the figurative, employing the formal term 'breast' (*mastou*) alongside innuendo suggestive of pubic hair.[34] The final results of drinking wine, Silenus notes, are more dancing and 'forgetting your troubles' (v. 172), concepts that are intimately connected to Dionysus and Dionysiac worship and religion.[35]

As Silenus exits into the cave to get the sheep and cheeses for Odysseus, he concludes his speech by asking rhetorically whether he should kiss the wine and tell the Cyclops and his eye to go weep (i.e. go to hell). During the discussion between Silenus and Odysseus, the satyrs do not speak any lines, but they were probably not passively observing the dialogue. Their tendencies in other satyr plays and their character in general suggest that they were relishing Silenus' enjoyment of the wine and enthusiastically supporting his comments on dance and sex, perhaps by mimicking some of the speech with outrageous stage action. If this is the case, the audience may have watched the members of the chorus dancing excitedly, diving onto the ground in feigned suicide (perhaps from the stage or a rock placed in the orchestra as a prop), and imitating sexual encounters, with some satyrs playing the role of Silenus while others played the role of the female being fondled. This stage action, which is not written into the text, would have provided some of the greatest humour in viewing the *Cyclops*.

When Silenus exits, the chorus leader forces Odysseus to endure a series of misogynistic jokes about Helen and women more generally. He asks if he and the other Greeks took Troy and Helen 'into hand' (v. 177), which Odysseus interprets through his heroic lens, affirming that, yes, the Greeks sacked the entire royal house. The chorus leader then asks if they all took turns 'banging' the young woman once they caught her, since she enjoys being married to many men. The term 'bang' (διεκροτήσατ᾽, 180) literally means to bore a hole in something, and is used metaphorically, though quite graphically, in the satyr's enquiry. He then calls Helen a traitor and describes her uncontrollable desire when she saw Paris' multicoloured pants and golden necklace. He also slights the Greek hero Menelaus by calling him a 'little man' (v. 185) and wraps up his speech by wishing that the entire race of women did not exist … except for satyrs alone.

Before Odysseus has an opportunity to respond, Silenus returns from the cave with a herd of bleating lambs and a number of cheeses for the Greek hero. He tells Odysseus and his men to give him the wine and flee quickly from the cave, but before the transaction can be completed, Silenus sees Polyphemus approaching. Everyone is at a loss. Silenus asks what they should do, and Odysseus asks where they should go. The elderly satyr suggests hiding in the cave because there are a number of hiding spots, a proposal that would bring the story in line with the Homeric version, but would make for a problematic theatrical production, since all the action would take place offstage. Euripides adapts the story by making Odysseus declare that Troy would groan if he fled a single man, since he fought so bravely against great hordes of men in Troy. His final remarks before Polyphemus' appearance onstage are a gnomic (and meta-mythological) sentiment: 'If dying is necessary, I will die nobly; or if I live, I will preserve my former reputation.'[36]

The Cyclops' entrance is just as thrilling as the satyrs' entrance, but instead of leaping dances and raucous song, Polyphemus dominates the stage with his larger-than-life, booming persona. As he walks onstage, holding a club in his hands, he bellows two powerful commands (v. 203), 'Hold up, make way!' His costume was probably equally commanding, with imposing size and style. Presumably, the largest actor available was given this role, and he would have worn a padded costume, some sort of lifts on his feet, and an oversized mask with a single eye in the centre. A Lucanian red-figure calyx crater (Figure 2.3) may give a sense of Polyphemus' appearance. Although Lucania is a region in Southern Italy, the fact that the artist painted the vase at roughly the same time as Euripides' *Cyclops* and includes satyrs in the Homeric scene suggests that Euripides' satyr play served as the main inspiration.[37] This is not to say that the vase offers a snapshot of the performance,[38] but it does provide our only visual depiction of Polyphemus that was (probably) based on a satyr play rather than another performance or the artist's imagination.[39] If nothing else, the vase may provide a sense of the original mask, which had two eyes for the actor to see through, but one giant eye in the middle of his forehead for the effect of a Cyclops.

Figure 2.3 The blinding of Polyphemus, Lucanian red-figure calyx crater, *c.* 420–410, attributed to the Cyclops Painter. British Museum, London, GR 1947.7-14.18.

After Polyphemus' initial commands, he turns to a string of questions, wondering what is going on, why the satyrs are being lazy, and why they are acting like Bacchants. Polyphemus' line of questions suggests that the satyrs were not merely milling about, but were engaging enthusiastically in traditional satyric dances. Much like Silenus at the choral parodos, Polyphemus observes the satyrs' actions and points out the disconnect between their religious, ritualistic dance and the absence of Dionysus: 'There is no Dionysus here, no rattles of bronze or beating drums' (vv. 204–5). Polyphemus injects Dionysus into the play through the negation of the Dionysiac. He wraps up his speech with questions about the status of his young lambs, his milk, and his cheese, but when he gets no response from the satyrs, he orders them to stop staring at the ground and threatens to hit them with his club if they do not answer him.

Polyphemus' command to the chorus to look up from the ground shows that although the satyrs were dancing raucously when he first came onstage, they stopped as soon as they spotted him. They obey the monster, saying that they have turned their heads to Zeus and the stars, that they are gazing upon Orion himself. Polyphemus asks a second time about his milk supply, and the satyrs inform him that there is both cow's and sheep's milk and a mixture of the two. They beg the monster not to devour them, and the Cyclops declares that the satyrs' leaping and dancing would be the death of him. Just then, he spots Odysseus and his men near the cave along with his lambs and buckets of cheese. He wonders if pirates or robbers have landed there, and he describes Silenus as an 'old man, with his bald head all swollen from blows/strokes' (v. 227). Polyphemus' description of Silenus indicates that the actor playing the satyr altered his appearance somehow when he went offstage to get the sheep. Silenus may have changed his mask so his face looked red and swollen from drinking too much wine, and since Polyphemus has never consumed wine himself, he incorrectly identifies the rosiness of the satyr's cheeks with the effects of being beaten by thieves.

A different interpretation of Polyphemus' language suggests that Euripides may have been making a sexual joke when Silenus re-emerged from the cave. The use of *phalakron* ('bald head', 227) had a history in satyr drama of indirectly referring to the satyrs' ithyphallicism, and the actor playing Silenus may have changed his

costume phallus from flaccid to erect while he was offstage. Although
phalakron literally means 'bald head', Richard Seaford has noted
the word's phonetic similarity to the Greek word for penis, and it
may even be a 'pun, brought out by intonation, on φαλλὸν ἄκρον',
signifying an erect penis.[40] In a fragment from Aeschylus' *Diktyulkoi*,
we see this same playful use of the word, when Silenus takes care of
the baby Perseus:

⟨ΣΙ.⟩]. γελᾷ μου προσορῶν
   ].. ὁ μικκὸς λιπαρὸν
   μ]ιλτ[ο]πρεπτον φαλακρὸν

                           Aeschylus *Diktyulkoi*, *TrGF* 47a 786–8

> The little one laughs when he looks at my oiled-up, bright red 'bald
> head'.

Despite the fragmentary state of these verses, the sexual imagery
in this passage is clear, and Aeschylus' postponed use of the double
entendre adds to the humour of the pun. The adjectives 'bright-
red' and 'oiled up', terms with sexual undertones, would anticipate
a reference to the satyr's phallus, but Silenus offers φαλακρόν (bald
head) instead of φαλλόν (phallus).[41] Polyphemus' language presents
the same opportunity for a joke, and Euripides intensifies the double
entendre when Polyphemus uses the ambiguous phrase 'swollen with
blows/strokes' (v. 227), which suggests that Silenus was masturbating
inside the cave after the wine helped him get an erection. If this is the
case, the actor would have probably changed his shorts while offstage
so that the costume phallus would be erect.

When Silenus hears Polyphemus' interpretation of the satyr's
physical change, he quickly adopts a pseudo-tragic tone, exclaiming
ômoi and telling the monster that he has received a terrible beating.
Again the language is vaguely sexual, perhaps indicating masturbation,
but Silenus quickly follows up by moaning that he was pummelled by
the foreigners because he tried to stop them from stealing Polyphemus'

cheeses and lambs. He even claims that the Greek men threatened to put Polyphemus in a dog collar, pull out his guts, flay his back with a whip, and bind his hands and feet so they could sell him as a slave. Silenus' imagination and lies are extraordinary, and his stage actions probably mimicked his words, as he acted all this out with gusto.

After Polyphemus hears Silenus' story, he calls to a servant (again, presumably extras dressed as satyrs) to go inside the cave, sharpen the knives, and start a fire so he can slaughter and cook the strangers. Polyphemus describes how he will have some bits of their flesh hot from the coals and boil the rest to tenderize it in his cauldron. He is tired of eating wild lion and deer and misses the flesh of men. Silenus encourages the monster, noting that a new menu tastes more pleasant after a stretch of ordinary food. Odysseus, however, speaks up and tells Polyphemus the truth: he and his men approached the cave wishing to buy food, and Silenus sold the sheep and cheese for wine. The melodrama in Silenus' response, 'Me?! May you be utterly destroyed!' (v. 261), is absurd. The satyr continues in this way, addressing Polyphemus as the 'most beautiful little Cyclops, [his] dear master' (v. 266), and swearing by Poseidon, Polyphemus' father, and a host of other sea entities (Triton, Nereus, Calypso, the Nereids, and the entire holy race of fish in the sea) that he was not trying to sell the monster's property. Silenus adds to the humour of his brazen lie by wishing that his own children, the chorus of satyrs whom he claims to love dearly die if he is lying.

The satyrs are quick to respond to Silenus' ridiculous oath and, rather nobly for satyrs, tell the truth to the Cyclops. They ask Polyphemus not to hurt the strangers, swearing that if they are lying, then their father should be destroyed. This entire scene between Silenus and the satyrs is humorous, especially when the Cyclops compares the old satyr to Rhadamanthys, a judge in the underworld who was known for being just. The association is so over the top that it is hard for the audience to give any credence to Polyphemus' ability to distinguish reality from fiction, or to see anyone for who he really is. The Cyclops changes the topic and asks Odysseus a handful of questions about his origins, questions which are considered inappropriate for the Greek custom of *xenia* and take on a much more perverse tone coming from Polyphemus than from Silenus. He compounds the cultural insult when he hears that Odysseus has been blown off course while returning from the Trojan War, calling the labour a shameful excursion, since the Greeks invaded a land for the sake of a single woman.

Odysseus responds to Polyphemus with one of his longest speeches in the play, an entreaty that is much more tragic and rhetorically adept than previous exchanges.[42] The first verse spoken by Odysseus is a straightforward statement claiming that a god, rather than a mortal, was the cause of the Trojan War. He then attempts to flatter Polyphemus, calling him the 'noble son of the god of the sea' (v. 286), and forcefully argues three separate points. First, he appeals to right and wrong, saying that he and his men should not serve as a godless meal for the Cyclops. Second, and more developed oratorically, is the argument that Odysseus and his men, through their suffering in the Trojan War, kept every part of Greece safe, including Polyphemus' island and Poseidon's temples. The third point made by Odysseus is that it is a custom amongst mortals to take care of shipwrecked men. They are to be given clothing and gifts of hospitality, not have their limbs pierced and roasted. Odysseus then appeals to sympathy, arguing that Troy has brought enough grief upon Greece. He paints a vivid picture of the bloodshed and scores of corpses in Troy, as well as the numerous widowed wives and childless elderly parents of slain soldiers in Greece. Odysseus' final petition is again to holiness, as he implores the Cyclops to choose godliness and give up shameful, impious meals and gluttony.

Although the mood on the stage would have probably been fairly sombre throughout Odysseus' speech, Silenus immediately undoes

Odysseus' efforts by advising Polyphemus to eat the hero's tongue so he too can become a clever chatterer. The satyrs, who had proven themselves supporters of the stranger, probably reacted with some form of sympathetic stage action, but it is the Cyclops who reacts with words. In a speech even longer than Odysseus', Polyphemus responds in legal, rhetorical fashion, listing the various reasons why he has no regard for the hero or holiness.[43] The speech reveals the Cyclops' sophistication in the Euripidean version of the story. He begins by mocking Odysseus' statement about the gods, saying that wealth is god to the wise man, while everything else is just chatter and fine sounding sentiments. He proceeds to point out that he simply does not care about his father Poseidon's temples, and he does not fear Zeus because he sees no way that the god is superior to himself. When Zeus rains, snows, and thunders, he nestles into his cave, provides himself a feast, drinks a jar of milk, wraps himself in animal skins, and starts a fire. To Polyphemus' surprisingly scientific and sophistic mind, Zeus is nothing more than the weather.[44] He sacrifices to no god but his belly, the greatest of all divinities. Polyphemus' philosophy is straightforward and modern: to eat and drink and suffer no pain is the best way of life.

Although Polyphemus' hedonistic views would have resonated with some members of the audience, there were certainly others who would find them appalling, and the Cyclops would be sure to alienate everyone as soon as he moved from the simple pleasure of eating and drinking to eating Odysseus and his men. The Cyclops orders the Greeks into the cave, and Odysseus offers a lament and a prayer to Athena, his patron throughout the Homeric epic. The tone he strikes is vastly different from that found in the *Odyssey* and remarkably similar to the sentiment found in Polyphemus' speech. He begs Athena to help him, since this danger is greater than that which he faced in Troy. He then implores Zeus Xenios (Protector of Guests) to look upon Polyphemus' injustices. The most intriguing portion of Odysseus' lament is his rebuke of Zeus, as he tells the god that if he does not acknowledge the Cyclops' crimes, he should be considered a 'useless god' (v. 355). Odysseus' harsh censure is just as impious as Polyphemus' speech about Zeus, and it is also similarly pragmatic. While many myths examine the unpredictability of the gods and the seeming inexplicability of human suffering, Odysseus offers an argument that is uncomplicated in its philosophy: why would Zeus Xenios, if he is a powerful god who protects the guest-host relationship, allow a foreigner and stranger to be harmed by a faithless and heartless Cyclops? If he does allow Odysseus to be harmed by Polyphemus, is Zeus a god worthy of worship at all? Euripides does not make these questions foremost in the *Cyclops*, but Odysseus mentions them more than once, which makes Odysseus appear agnostic at best or atheistic at worst. Members of the audience, whether they tolerated these ideas or found them reprehensible, were aware that certain philosophers in Athens advocated these beliefs.[45] As the first episode comes to a close, Euripides has brought the audience on a turbulent ride, exposing them to obscene humour, first-class oratorical technique, melodrama, vibrant song and dance, tense stichomythia, tragic dialogue, and philosophical and religious ideas.

First stasimon (356–74)

While Polyphemus ushers the Greek sailors into the cave, the chorus of satyrs begins a brief song and dance that describes the Cyclops' gruesome actions and their desire to take no part in them. During the stasimon, the stage would have been absent of everyone but the chorus, and the metre and song, although traditional, would have been powerful, particularly with the vivid imagery that the satyrs offer.[46] They address the Cyclops directly, even though he is not onstage, telling him to open his throat since 'The limbs of the foreigners are boiled and broiled and warm from the coals, ready for you to gnaw, devour, and chop' (vv. 357–9). At the end of this quote, the satyrs pile verb on top of verb without conjunction (asyndeton), which contrasts their overuse of conjunctions when describing the methods used for cooking the flesh. The satyrs use the term *xenos* in a prominent position at the end of the thought. This is the first of three uses of the word in this short choral song, showing again the importance of the theme of guest-host relationships to the Homeric myth and the Euripidean satyr play.

The satyrs' mesode (the portion of the choral ode between strophe and antistrophe) continues the second person address to the Cyclops, but they switch to imperative commands: 'Just don't, don't give any to me' (v. 361). The satyrs stress the singularity of Polyphemus' crime, repeating that he alone fills his vessel and he does it only for himself. The metaphor of filling a ship is unique and fitting—Polyphemus is a giant stuffing himself with cargo, not eating by any appropriate Greek definition of the term. As the song proceeds to the antistrophe, there are some textual problems in our manuscript tradition, including the inversion, it seems, of two lines and the loss of another.[47] Nevertheless, the tone and message are clear. The chorus calls the Cyclops a pitiless wretch who sacrifices strangers/ guests who have come as suppliants to his altar. This ode is located at the half-way point in the play, and stresses the thematically central issues of sacrifice and the guest-host relationship. To conclude their song, the satyrs return to the shocking imagery of Polyphemus tearing, feasting, and devouring the boiled and roasted flesh with his foul teeth. This short song would have been moving, with its grisly, sacrilegious, yet poetic descriptions, and although we do not know much about choral dance, it is reasonable to assume that the satyrs' choreographed movements would have reflected the powerful imagery as they performed onstage alone.

Second episode (375–607)

Unlike Homer, Euripides uses no giant boulder to block the entrance-way of Polyphemus' cave, an element of the *Cyclops* that changes the story significantly, but is necessary because of the limitations of the stage. As the satyrs complete their first stasimon, Odysseus appears from the cave and asks a somewhat surprising rhetorical question, considering his recent questioning of the gods. He calls upon Zeus, asking the god what he can possibly say after seeing such terrible and unbelievable things. He calls Polyphemus' actions the stuff of myths, and the leader of the chorus asks Odysseus how he could endure such a fate. In his answer, one of the play's longest speeches, he covers a lot of ground, from a detailed description of the events in the cave to his escape outdoors. The first half of Odysseus' oration is a meticulous account of everything that happened upon entering Polyphemus' house: the Cyclops piles up enough oak logs to load three wagons, starts a fire, spreads a bed of fir branches on the ground, and sets about ninety gallons of milk next to a massive five-foot-wide cup made of ivy wood. The description of Polyphemus' preparation for the meal is exhaustive, and the particular details that Odysseus focuses on consistently stress Polyphemus' size and strength. Odysseus' account would have helped inspire the imaginations of audience members, since costuming could not fully accomplish the sense of such a monstrously oversized character. When Odysseus moves on to describe the more gruesome elements of the meal's preparation, he remains focused on minutiae. Polyphemus snatches up two of Odysseus' men and drains the blood of one into the cauldron by slitting his throat; then he smashes the head of the other, emptying his brains on the rocks. The monster butchers the men, roasts the fleshy parts, and throws the arms and legs into a cauldron.

This section is fascinating for a couple reasons. First, Euripides seems to present a Polyphemus with far more developed culinary interests than we find in the Homeric version.[48] Odysseus describes cooking methods and cooking devices in great detail in the *Cyclops*, but Homer avoids such specifics; in fact, the Homeric monster does not even cook his meal.[49] The second point of interest is that

Odysseus admits to assisting Polyphemus in this 'wretchedness' (v. 406). Although Odysseus says he wept uncontrollably, he also notes that he helped Polyphemus prepare the feast, but he never explains why. The audience may suspect that this is part of the hero's plan to trick the monster, but as he notes in the final section of the speech, a divinely inspired idea came to him only after Polyphemus ate and collapsed on the floor. Euripides leaves the audience wondering if Odysseus is entirely self-serving, as the hero proceeds to delineate his plot to get Polyphemus drunk on the 'divine drink, the pride of Dionysus' (v. 415). In the cave, the hero offered the Cyclops cup after cup of wine until he was intoxicated and began to sing an out-of-tune song. Odysseus' men continue to cower and weep in the cave, while Odysseus sneaks out to ask for the satyrs' assistance in leaving the island. Silenus is too drunk to help, but if the members of the chorus are willing to offer their service, Odysseus says he will get them back to their old friend Dionysus.

The satyrs enthusiastically agree to help the hero, but rather than focusing on Dionysus, as Odysseus has done, they once again focus on satisfying their desires, stating that they cannot wait to escape because their 'siphon' has long been 'widowed' (vv. 439–40). Euripides abruptly shifts the tone of the play, moving from the horrific events of the cave to the excitement of escape and finally to the satyrs' hope of sexual pleasure. The joke was presumably accompanied by a similar shift in the satyrs' attitude and action, as they danced and stroked their stage phalluses with the mention of their 'siphons'.[50] Odysseus pays no attention to the satyrs' puerile stunts, but instead begins to explain his plan to help them escape. The satyrs, who have heard of Odysseus' crafty nature, are eager to hear the plan. He says that Polyphemus wants to go revel with his brothers, and that they must prevent it. There is a good deal of telegraphing here, since this scene is about to take place onstage, but the narrative elements substitute for the parts that will have to take place even later in the cave. Odysseus says he will tell Polyphemus not to share the wine, since it offers a life of pleasure. Then, when the giant is 'conquered by Dionysus' (v. 454), he will stab and melt the Cyclops' eye with an olive-wood stake sharpened and heated in a fire. At this point, Odysseus employs the same memorable simile that Homer (*Odyssey* 9.381) used to describe these events: just as a shipbuilder twirls a drill, he will whirl the stake into the Cyclops' eye socket and singe his eye.

The chorus is maddened with joy at the prospect of harming Polyphemus, shouting unintelligible sounds and even asking if they can aid in the carnage. Odysseus tells the satyrs that they have to help because the olive tree is so large. They respond with typical satyric braggadocio, saying they could lift a hundred wagons worth of weight, so long as they get to burn out the Cyclops' eye. As Odysseus slips back into Polyphemus' cave, he tells them to be quiet. The chorus leader asks who will line up first to grind out the monster's eye, but he quickly silences the rest of the group when Polyphemus drunkenly exits his home, singing an off-key tune.

As the Cyclops stumbles onto the stage, the chorus leader orders his fellow satyrs to educate Polyphemus in revels, and the satyrs sing (vv. 495–502):

> Blessed is he who shouts the Bacchic cry,
> as he gives himself over to the revel,
> possessed by the beloved streams of the grapes.
> Blessed is he who embraces his dear friend
> and who has a voluptuous escort—
> a sweet flower upon his bed—
> who has curls oiled with myrrh
> and calls, 'Who will open the door for me?'

This strophe contains perhaps the most significant verses of the entire play, both religiously and for the plot. By educating the uneducated monster in religious, Bacchic revelry, the satyrs express the most important elements of Dionysiac worship. These lines also function, though, as the turning point in the play, when Polyphemus (much like Pentheus in Euripides' *Bacchae*[51]) becomes initiated into Dionysiac religion. He sings and dances in direct response to the chorus, saying he is full of wine and cheer and wishes to revel with his brothers. Polyphemus' change of heart also alters the tone of the play somewhat from the Homeric original. His consumption of Dionysus, in the form of wine, has initiated him into the Dionysiac *thiasos* (group of worshippers), and he offers a scenario in which Odysseus, his comrades, and the satyrs could escape without any further danger to the hero or the satyrs. If Odysseus were to let the Cyclops go celebrate Dionysus with his fellow Cyclopes, all the men and satyrs could flee together without further destruction, but Odysseus' need for retribution makes this easy escape out of the question. The satyrs appear to be on-board with Odysseus retributive justice, as they sing in the third strophe that Polyphemus will be crowned with more than one type of wreath around his head, alluding to the injury that the Cyclops will soon suffer at the hands of Odysseus.

For the next sixty lines, there is another fast-paced stichomythic exchange between Odysseus, Polyphemus, and, in the second half, Silenus. The hero and monster discuss the god Dionysus. Polyphemus wonders how and why the god lives inside a wineskin, and repeatedly extols the benefits of sharing the wine with his brothers in a revel. Odysseus lies to him, though, telling him he will be more honoured if he keeps the wine for himself, and that revels end in fist-fights and quarrels. The use of the religious language *kômos* (revel) clearly indicates that Polyphemus has been initiated into the cult of Dionysus, and when Odysseus advises him again to stay, Polyphemus expresses a Dionysiac sentiment that would please an Athenian audience at the City Dionysia: 'Foolish is the man who drinks but does not love a revel' (v. 537). The Cyclops' Dionysian transformation is complete, but he ultimately turns to Silenus for advice. The precise language in these verses is uncertain because of textual problems,[52] but the Cyclops is finally convinced to lie down on the soft, flowery earth and drink alone.

Immediately, the scene turns towards humorous shtick, as Silenus repeatedly moves the wine and steals sips while no one is looking. This section would have been entertaining to watch, with the Cyclops lying on the ground and Silenus sneaking about filching wine. It also includes the crucial moment in which the Cyclops asks Odysseus his name. Odysseus, of course, tells Polyphemus that his name is Noman (*Outis*, v. 549), and the monster offers him a guest-host gift: to be eaten last of all his men. This confirms Polyphemus' immorality, despite his newfound appreciation for Dionysus. Silenus continues to steal the wine with various excuses and schemes (about a half dozen times total), before Polyphemus puts Odysseus in charge of pouring the wine. When the Cyclops begins to feel drunk, seeing the earth and sky blurring together, he says he is going to go to bed with Silenus, his 'Ganymede' (v. 582). The elderly satyr has functioned as a wine-pourer (the role of Ganymede amongst the gods), but his age makes him very unlike the young boy who also served as Zeus' lover.[53] The comparison would have been funny to the audience, but not to Silenus, whom Polyphemus drags into the cave for a forced sexual encounter.

When Silenus and the Cyclops exit the stage, Odysseus calls upon the satyrs to be men, since the stake is ready and Polyphemus will soon fall asleep. The chorus leader responds in mock-heroic tone that the satyrs' resolve is like stone or adamant, and they call upon the hero to go inside and rescue their father before he is sexually assaulted by the giant. Before exiting, Odysseus prays to the god of the forge, Hephaestus, who as the god of volcanoes is also the lord of Mt. Aetna, where the play takes place. The hero asks the god to burn out the eye of the monster. He then implores the deified form of Sleep to strike the monster with slumber so they can stab him and escape. The speech ends with another harsh ultimatum to the gods: if Odysseus and his men die at the hands of such a savage, then Chance should be considered a greater divinity than the Olympian deities. Odysseus does not explore these sentiments again in the play, but the fact that he mentions them both times he exits the stage would have highlighted the hero's somewhat irreverent tone in the play.

Second stasimon (608–24)

Odysseus briefly enters the cave, and the chorus performs another short song and dance. They foreshadow the loss of the guest-eater's eye and offer a vivid depiction of the firebrand, huge and burning, sitting in the ashes. They pray for Maron's wine to come, act, and remove Polyphemus' eye so that he will regret drinking. This is striking given the satyrs' own constant desire to drink and Polyphemus' somewhat admirable desire to take part in Dionysiac ritual. However, for the satyrs, Odysseus, and the Athenian audience, Polyphemus' crimes cannot be undone. Odysseus (or perhaps more appropriately, Dionysus) has forced the Cyclops to become an initiate of the god because of his transgressions, rather than as an opportunity for religious redemption. The chorus concludes its song with a prayer to leave the Cyclops' lonely land and again see ivy-garlanded Dionysus.

Third episode (625–53)

When Odysseus reappears, he angrily commands the chorus of 'wild beasts' (v. 625) to close their mouths and be quiet. He orders them not to breathe or blink or cough in hopes that the Cyclops will stay asleep. The satyrs would have presumably made over the top attempts to be motionless, perhaps holding physically ridiculous, exaggerated positions while Odysseus berates them. The precise attribution of lines here is challenging, but it is clear that the chorus is physically divided onstage and that none of the members of the chorus is particularly eager to take on Polyphemus. One choral member says that the satyrs are holding their breath, at which point Odysseus orders them to go inside and grab the fiery stake. But another satyr responds that his group is standing too far from the cave's entrance and cannot push the firebrand into the Cyclops' eye. A third satyr then claims that his group has gone lame, and a fourth says that he has suffered the same fate: he has just sprained his ankle while standing still. Then, 'somehow', their eyes are suddenly full of dust and ash. The pantomime throughout this scene would have been amusing, as the members of the chorus go from standing still and holding their breath to having sprained ankles and dust in their eyes.

Odysseus, annoyed and impatient to get back inside, calls the satyrs worthless cowards, and they compound their cowardly nature by asking, 'Just because I feel sorry for my back and my spine, and just because I don't want him to knock out my teeth, I'm a coward' (vv. 643–5)? From a technical point of view, the satyrs cannot leave the stage to assist in this task, since the chorus would be expected to stay onstage throughout the play.[54] Euripides playfully alludes to these restrictions when his satyrs say that they stand too far from the Cyclops to stab out his eye. In the end, though, the satyrs turn their cowardice (and the constraints of theatrical expectations) into a moment of religious piety. They swear that they know an Orphic song so wondrous that the stake will walk up to the Cyclops on its own and set him on fire.

Third stasimon (654–62)

Although the degree of assistance provided by the satyrs' song is never fully addressed, the magical elements of the third stasimon are important. Odysseus says that he has always known that the satyrs were cowards, and that he must now stab the Cyclops' eye with his companions alone. But he does not merely disappear into the cave—he also orders the satyrs to cheer him and his men on as they punish Polyphemus. When the hero exits, the chorus sings a fascinating song with elements suggestive of religious ritual, but it is hard to know whether the incantation would have been interpreted as serious or humorous. The satyrs begin with untranslatable shouts and then order an unspecified subject (presumably Odysseus and his crew) to burn out the eye of the beast, and to whirl and pull the stake so the Cyclops cannot harm them. The language is ritualistic, with their Dionysiac 'Io, Io', and eight imperative forms within seven short lines. The performance of this scene would have been an extraordinary spectacle, with the stage empty of all characters and attention focused entirely on the dancing, mimicking, singing chorus.

Fourth episode and exodos (663–709)

The satyrs' song is ended by the appearance of Polyphemus from the cave. The giant shouts *ômoi*, an exclamation of surprise, pain, and horror, because his eye has been completely burned out. The actor playing the Cyclops would have changed his mask to reflect the damage inflicted by Odysseus and his men, and the eye socket would be bloodied, singed, and vacant. There would probably be blood dripping down the mask and perhaps even the costume. Despite the horror, the immediate effect would primarily be humour. In fact, the satyrs are so ecstatic when they see Polyphemus that they ask him to repeat his words of pain. The Cyclops obliges and again shouts *ômoi*, before reflecting on the injustices he has suffered. He then roars to the Greek men that they will never escape the cave since he will take a stand at the entrance and block it with his hands.

Throughout this fast-paced scene, most characters rattle off single or half lines in quick succession. The chorus asks the Cyclops what the problem is, and when he responds that he is destroyed, they tell him that he does look ugly. In 'Who's on first' style, the satyrs ask the monster if he got so drunk that he fell into the coals, and he responds that (vv. 672–5):

> Cy: Noman destroyed me.
>   Ch: So no one has injured you.
> Cy: Noman blinded me, right in the eyelid.
>   Ch: So, you're not blind?
>   ...[55]
>
>   Ch: How could no one blind you?
> Cy: You're making fun of me. Where is Noman?
>   Ch: Nowhere, Cyclops.

At this point, Polyphemus explains that it was the guest/foreigner who has destroyed him with wine, to which the satyrs respond that wine is indeed *deinos*, an adjective that can mean both awful and awesome or terrible and tremendous. When the Cyclops asks if the Greeks have fled, the chorus leader tells the giant that they are hiding under a rocky overhang, and after more banter they lead the blind monster to the side so Odysseus, the sailors, and (presumably) Silenus can sneak out of the cave.[56] They also manage to guide Polyphemus into a jutting rock, where he smashes his already injured head. The satyrs continue to steer Polyphemus in circles, until the giant realizes that they are tricking him, and he shouts *oimoi gelômai* (v. 687), 'Ah, you're laughing at me!'

The satyrs persist in their abuse of Polyphemus until Odysseus reveals his location and his name. Polyphemus is perplexed and stops suddenly, so Odysseus explains that the Cyclops was destined to pay for his unholy meal. The play comes abruptly to an end as Polyphemus remembers a prophecy that foretold he would one day be blinded by a man named Odysseus, and he also notes that the hero has been prophesied to suffer at sea as punishment. Odysseus says that he is heading to launch his ship back home, and as Polyphemus exits the stage through the cave, he tells Odysseus that the Greek men will not escape, that he will break off a piece of the mountain and crush them all. After the Cyclops has exited, the satyrs conclude the play with a final couplet that both wraps up the plot and injects a final element of Dionysian religion. They say they will be the fellow sailors of Odysseus and slaves to Bacchus for the rest of time.

Themes, Issues, and Functions

In the *Cyclops*, Euripides presents a theatrical version of one of the most famous scenes from Homer's *Odyssey*, but it is not a simple adaptation of an archaic myth.[1] Euripides manipulates the Homeric plot to fit important themes of satyr drama, and to draw particular social, religious, and historical connections to Athens. In this chapter, we will see that Euripides updates Homer's *Odyssey* so it becomes more relevant for an audience at the fifth-century City Dionysia. Not only does he establish the play as a vehicle for Dionysiac religious worship, but he also engages with the satyric trope of meta-performance, using formal performative language throughout the play. He then reinforces the genre's role as Dionysiac worship by relating this metatheatrical language back to Dionysus.[2] We will also see that Euripides revises the myth by adding various references to contemporary Athenian philosophy and history. Odysseus and Polyphemus become complex figures, not simple Homeric representations of the 'civilized vs. uncivilized'. The Cyclops becomes a rather sympathetic gourmand with contemporary Athenian philosophical views, and Odysseus becomes a somewhat cruel figure who questions the existence and power of the gods in the manner of fifth-century Athenian sophists. Euripides even relocates the play to Sicily, where Athens had recently (if our dating of the play is correct) suffered a devastating military loss, aligning the hero Odysseus with the Athenians and the monster Polyphemus with the Sicilians. The *Cyclops*, it turns out, has much more to do with the audience's world than the mythological world from which the story was drawn.

'Nothing to do with Dionysus'

As we saw in the first chapter, satyr drama was apparently instituted at
the Athenian City Dionysia because the plots of early tragedy moved
beyond the purely Dionysian, and spectators were vocal in their
complaints that these performances had 'Nothing to do with Dionysus'.
Satyr drama, with its constant chorus of Dionysian companions, re-
established a distinct connection to the god.[3] Euripides' *Cyclops*, as
the only complete satyr play from antiquity, offers an opportunity to
test the connections between satyr drama and the 'Nothing to do with
Dionysus' legend.[4] As we will see, Euripides clearly and repeatedly
provides connections to the god, even though Dionysus never appears
in the play as a character. From a statistical point of view, the number
of references to the god is astonishing, given that the play is only a
little over 700 lines long. The name *Bacchios* is used twelve times,[5]
Bromios is mentioned six times, and *Dionysos* five, which averages out
to about one mention of the god in every thirty lines. In addition to
the direct references to Dionysus, there are also a range of references
to Dionysiac ritual and mythology: Bacchic worship (βακχιάζετε,
204, 'to celebrate Bacchus'; εὐίων βακχευμάτων, 25, 'Bacchic frenzy';
εὐιάζει, 495 'to shout in honor of Bacchus'), the companions of the
god (Βάκχαι, 'Bacchants', Νύμφαι, 'Nymphs'), and a host of other
Dionysiac references (e.g. 'Bacchic grapes', 192; Dionysian 'drums', 65;
and the 'wineskin', in which the god dwells, 525–30).

Throughout the *Cyclops*, Euripides never allows his audience to
forget Dionysus; in fact, he mentions him prominently in the three
most important sections of the play – the prologue, the choral entrance
(*eisodos*), and the choral exit (*exodos*). Silenus is the first character to
come onstage, and in a typically Euripidean introductory prologue,[6]
he provides a lengthy description of the trials that he has encountered
both with and on account of Dionysus. His very first words in the
first verse of the play are addressed to the god: 'Oh, Bromius!!' Then,

directly after Silenus' Dionysiac-themed introduction, the chorus bounds onto the stage from the side entrance, and the elderly satyr narrates their action. He cannot believe that his children are dancing and celebrating just as they did in their former revels with the god, and when the satyrs sing their entrance song, they point out that Dionysus is absent from the land of the Cyclopes:

> οὐ τάδε Βρόμιος, οὐ τάδε χοροὶ
> Βακχεῖαι τε θυρσοφόροι,
> οὐ τυμπάνων ἀλαλαγ-
> μοί, κρήναις παρ' ὑδροχύτοις,
> οὐκ οἴνου χλωραὶ σταγόνες
> οὐδ' ἐν Νύσα μετὰ Νυμ-
> φᾶν ἴακχον ἴακχον ᾠ-
> δὰν μέλπω πρὸς τὰν Ἀφροδί-
> ταν, ἃν θηρεύων πετόμαν
> Βάκχαις σὺν λευκόποσιν.

Euripides, Cyclops 63–73

There is no Bromius here, no choruses here,
no Thyrsus-bearing Bacchants,
no din of drums
beside gushing springs,
no juicy drops of wine.
Nor do I sing with the nymphs
on Mount Nysa the song 'Iacchus, Iacchus'
to Aphrodite,
whom I used to dart after, hunting
alongside the white-footed Bacchants.

The satyrs complain that there are none of the typical elements of their Dionysiac revel on the island of the Cyclopes, but the ode functions as a paralepsis of sorts: by longing for these Dionysiac features, they actually emphasize them more than if they were merely part of the performance. In addition, they fail to recognize the irony that their desire for Dionysiac song and dance is in fact delivered in a Dionysiac song and dance. Then, at the end of the play, as the chorus of satyrs exit the stage, they sing one final couplet (708–9), exclaiming that they 'will be slaves to Bacchus for the rest of time'. So, in addition to being mentioned, on average, approximately every thirty lines, Dionysus is also referred to during the moments in the production that are the most marked in terms of transition and formal importance, which lends a special weight to the god's role in the play.

In addition to the technical and religious language used in relation to Silenus and the satyrs, Euripides also uses a surprising amount of Dionysiac terminology in contexts directly related to the ogre, Polyphemus.[7] In fact, the Cyclops comes across somewhat as a Dionysiac character even before he is introduced to the god. He bangs his milk pail (323–8) as if it is a Dionysian tympanum, and he wears the hides of animals (329–31) and wanders through the wilderness as Dionysiac worshippers do, including the satyrs themselves. And despite his atheistic, even anti-theistic speeches, Polyphemus becomes a traditional worshipper of Dionysus. In fact, the play reaches its Dionysian zenith after the Cyclops has had his first taste of wine, which metonymically represents the god Dionysus himself. The monster consumes the wine (and, thus, the god) and becomes more in touch with Dionysus, appreciating his divine power and even realizing how and why he should be venerated as a god. As Polyphemus symbolically becomes an initiate in the god's religion through the consumption of wine, he acts more Dionysian, to the point that he wants to share the drink and revel with the other Cyclopes in a traditional Dionysian *kômos*.[8]

When Polyphemus is exposed to Dionysus' wine and becomes an initiate, he also becomes a slave of the god.[9] Euripides explores this theme throughout the play by juxtaposing voluntary slavery to Dionysus and involuntary slavery to Polyphemus.[10] As prisoners of Polyphemus, the satyrs are forced to serve the Cyclops, but they desire to serve Dionysus and are, therefore, eventually freed. In fact, it could be argued that they are free even during their enslavement to the monster, since they sing and dance just as they formerly did with the god. Polyphemus, however, rejects and refuses to serve Dionysus, which ultimately results in the Cyclops (a free 'man' who forces slavery on others) to be forced into slavery to the god. Much like Euripides' *Bacchae*, the *Cyclops* suggests that anyone who willingly becomes a slave of Dionysus and worships the god will be honoured and saved.[11] Those who reject the god will be forced to worship him in a perverted way that will eventually lead to severe pain and suffering, or even death. The *Cyclops* instructs its audience that all mankind will ultimately be a slave to Dionysus, but those who take on this role willingly will experience freedom, escape their troubles, and even be reborn beyond the pains of this world.[12]

Self-awareness of performance

Satyr drama was uniquely repetitive at the City Dionysia. Each year, there were tragedies and comedies at the festival, but the choruses of these genres continually changed. No matter what myth was presented in a satyr play, though, there was (almost) always a chorus of satyrs.[13] With three satyr choruses brought onstage every year, satyrs could be considered the one constant at the festival. For the spectator, actor, author, and even for Silenus and the chorus, each satyr play would have blended into all other performances of satyr drama in a way that was not true of tragedy or comedy.[14] This created a performative fusion that helped make satyr drama a particularly self-reflective genre, where authors were not only engaging with earlier literary sources of the myth being presented, but were also engaging with all other earlier satyr plays. Poets of satyr drama highlighted this intra-generic relationship by making their plays self-consciously performative, an approach that reached its peak (in extant satyr play) with Astydamas the Younger's culinary metaphor.[15] One of Astydamas' characters uses a parabatic style to express that poets must please the audience just as a chef pleases diners.[16] Although Euripides is not so unrestrained in the *Cyclops*, he does underscore his play's own 'play-ness'.[17] As we detail some of the overtly performative elements of the *Cyclops*, we will see that the generic, metatheatrical self-awareness actually relates back to Dionysian themes noted in the previous section.[18]

At the start of the play, Silenus presents an introductory monologue that is imbued with a certain awareness of the play's existence in the tradition of satyr plays, as well as the elderly satyr's role in that tradition. Of particular note is Silenus' claim to have undertaken 'countless labors' (*murious ponous*, v. 1) alongside and on behalf of Dionysus. He says that he assisted Dionysus when Hera drove him mad and again when the Olympian gods battled the Giants, but that nothing compares to his current predicament, which began when Dionysus was kidnapped by Tyrrhenian pirates. These storylines and the 'countless' other unnamed labours naturally evoke the plots of previous satyr plays.[19] By the time of Euripides' *Cyclops*, there had been hundreds of satyr plays performed in the same location, at the same time of year, at the same festival. And Silenus had starred in every single one of these performances.[20] As a character in three plays per year at the Greater Dionysiac festival, Silenus—like the chorus of satyrs—is in constant conversation with himself, whether the poet draws attention to this conversation, as Euripides does here, or whether the poet makes no particular effort to highlight the intra-generic relationship. There is no escaping the perpetual dialogue between the City Dionysia's multiple satyr plays, multiple Silenuses, and multiple satyr choruses from the past, present, and future. Silenus rummages through previous versions of satyric stories, naming common *topoi* of satyr play, and pointing out the various missions he has completed as a permanent character on the Athenian stage.

Euripides follows up Silenus' metatheatrical introduction with a number of meta-performative moments in the *Cyclops*, and much like Silenus' prologue, each instance focuses on Dionysus and the Dionysiac. The most obvious example is found just as the chorus is entering the stage for the first time:

ἤδη δὲ παῖδας προσνέμοντας εἰσορῶ
ποίμνας. τί ταῦτα; μῶν κρότος σικινίδων
ὁμοῖος ὑμῖν νῦν τε χῶτε Βακχίωι
κῶμος συνασπίζοντες ᾿Αλθαίας δόμους
προσῆιτ᾿ ἀοιδαῖς βαρβίτων σαυλούμενοι;

Euripides, *Cyclops* 36–40

Now I see my sons goading the flocks this way.
What is going on here? Surely, children, this is not the same beat
of the *sikinnis* that you struck during your campaign for Bacchus,
back when you traveled as a band of revelers to the house of
    Althaea
and strutted along to the songs of the Dionysiac lyre?

Silenus' pronouncement of the choral parodos focuses attention on the satyrs' Dionysiac dancing, which he compares to their earlier mythological experiences, when they went 'strutting' or 'swaggering' in revel with Dionysus to the halls of Althaea.[21] As the satyrs dance onto the stage, Silenus draws upon Dionysiac myth, but he also draws upon actual Dionysiac performances, naming the *sikinnis*, a dance singularly associated with satyrs.[22] Festa, in his thorough study of the satyric dance, examines a mass of literary and artistic evidence and draws certain conclusions about the precise elements of the *sikinnis*: the satyrs move in a semicircular motion, while alternately raising their right leg and arm and then their left leg and arm.[23] Silenus does not merely say that the satyrs are dancing and swaggering onto stage. He explicitly names the official, formal dance of satyrs, as they enter and perform that dance for the audience and Dionysus. This sort of metatheatrical reflection comes very close to breaking dramatic illusion, as Silenus draws attention to the chorus' own 'chorus-ness'.

In this same passage, Silenus uses another technical term, *kômos* (revel), which is not quite as formal as *sikinnis*, but again directs attention to the play's relation to performance, especially within the larger historical context of satyr drama.[24] As we will see in the following chapter, satyr play appears to have, at least in part, grown out of dithyrambic *kômos*-song.[25] Various komasts (performers of the *kômos*) are conflated with satyrs during the archaic period: they are presented in the same mythological contexts, they are often associated with Dionysus, and they are similarly 'phallic' in their presentation.[26] Komasts also begin to disappear on visual representations just as satyrs become much more popular, which suggests not only that komasts and satyrs have an intimate relationship in Greek performance and ritual, but that satyrs may even have taken over the role of komasts in Dionysiac, dithyrambic performance.[27]

The early history of komastic and satyric performance is chronologically a long way off from the date of the *Cyclops*, but the number of times that Euripides mentions the *kômos* in his play suggests that he is engaging with satyr drama's formal connections to komastic productions (and, presumably, the Dionysiac elements that accompany the *kômos*).[28] In fact, of the 16 extant tragedies of Euripides (comprising more than 23,000 lines of poetry), *kômos* is used only eight times, but in the approximately seven hundred lines of Euripides' *Cyclops*, it is used seven times.[29] These statistics suggest a purposeful association between his satyr play and the *kômos*, and the context of the various uses reinforces the term's importance in the play. In addition to Silenus' use during the choral parodos, Polyphemus wants to go revel with his brothers after his first sips of wine (445), but Odysseus says the monster must be kept from such a revel (451), and when the Cyclops comes back onstage, the satyr chorus uses the term twice in its self-exhortation:

φέρε νυν κώμοις παιδεύσωμεν
τὸν ἀπαίδευτον·

...

μάκαρ ὅστις εὐιάζει
βοτρύων φίλαισι πηγαῖς
ἐπὶ κῶμον ἐκπετασθεὶς

Euripides, *Cyclops* 492–7

Come on, let us educate
the untrained man in our revels.

...

Blessed is he who shouts the Bacchic cry,
as he gives himself over to the revel,
possessed by the beloved streams of the grapes.

The religious elements are clear, as the chorus sings that Dionysiac revellers who celebrate with wine and friends are blessed. When Polyphemus wishes to join the revel (508), however, Odysseus prevents him, saying that the *kômos* leads to fighting (534). The last mention of the term (537) occurs during Polyphemus' final attempt to embrace the Dionysian revel, as he fully transforms into a worshipper of the god and criticizes anyone who drinks but does not participate in the *kômos*. Six of the seven uses of the term are concentrated within Polyphemus' initiation scene, and the only other occurrence is during the choral parodos. This demonstrates the term's religious importance in the play and the connection between the performative elements of the satyrs and Polyphemus. The satyrs offer appropriate Dionysiac, komastic performance, and the Cyclops, after being taken over by the god, wants to be a performer as well, but his fate as Dionysian victim has been sealed.[30]

    In addition to the religious and performative terminology of *sikinnis* and *kômos*, Euripides also connects Dionysiac ritual and performance with various meta-poetic references to song and dance.[31] For example, shortly after Silenus' performative references in the prologue, the chorus dances onstage and engages in a similarly playful version of self-referentiality, as they announce that οὐ τάδε Βρόμιος, οὐ τάδε χοροὶ (There is no Bromius here, no choruses). The sentiment is both humorous and metatheatrical. As the satyrs sing these verses and claim that Dionysus is not present, they are literally standing in the orchestra at the Theater of Dionysus, before a representation of the god Dionysus himself.[32] Even more amusingly, they sing and dance as a chorus, while asserting that there are no choruses on the island of the Cyclopes.[33] The metatheatrical playfulness is further highlighted by the fact that the satyrs are a group of men trained to perform as a formal chorus, and they use the formal language *choroi*. Then, when Silenus gets his first taste of wine since being stranded in Sicily, he uses the official language of dancing in a chorus (χορεῦσαι) at the Dionysiac festival, shouting 'Ba-Bae! Bacchus is beckoning me to dance. Ah, ah, ah!' (156–7). Even Polyphemus, when he enters the stage, engages in formal allusions to performance, complaining (204), 'Why are you dancing for Bacchus? There is no Dionysus here.' The verb βακχιάζω means 'to celebrate the mysteries of Bacchus', and suggests an official, ritual dance/performance in honour of the god. Polyphemus, a monster with supposedly no knowledge of Dionysus, walks onstage and, upon seeing the dancing satyrs, asks why they are performing a Bacchic dance.

As these various examples show, Euripides repeatedly presents satyric song and dance as a religious performance, drawing attention to the *Cyclops*' own performative elements by using formal language of the theatre. He also amplifies the Dionysian nature of these meta-references by employing formal language related to ritual performance. And Euripides' repeated references to the Dionysian *kômos* also place the *Cyclops* in dialogue with satyr drama's own literary and religious performative history. Satyr drama functioned as ritualized Dionysiac revelry that developed from earlier non-theatrical Dionysiac performance, and the satyrs take part in the *kômos* of satyr play as soon as they enter the stage. Then, when Polyphemus is introduced to Dionysus in the form of wine, the focus turns exclusively to the revel. Polyphemus wants to be a 'good' initiate and celebrate the god with his brothers, but Odysseus distracts him in order to achieve his revenge.[34] Using religious and meta-theatrical language, Euripides presents his *Cyclops* as a performance for Dionysus, showing clearly that satyr drama had 'something to do with Dionysus'.

Xenia, barbarism, and philosophy

In addition to the religious and metatheatrical elements found in the *Cyclops*, Euripides also develops certain themes and issues that are particular to the myth of Odysseus (and are therefore found in Homer's *Odyssey*), but he tends to manipulate them in a way that makes them more complex and relevant to the time and place of the satyric performance.[35] The main theme that Euripides adopts from the Homeric original is the concept of *xenia*, the ancient notion of reciprocal hospitality: kindness and generosity should be granted to strangers by potential hosts and, in turn, kindness and generosity should be granted to hosts who protect and care for strangers.[36] Sometimes this hospitality was articulated by offering simple human necessities, such as clothing, food, and shelter, and other times it was expressed with the exchange of material gifts and treasured personal possessions. The theme of *xenia* is one of the most prominent motifs found in archaic poetry, and after 'homecoming' it is arguably the most dominant theme of Homer's *Odyssey*. Odysseus' entire journey is punctuated by encounters with good hosts (e.g. the Phaeacians and the swineherd Antinous) and bad hosts (e.g. Circe and Calypso), but the negative paradigm of *xenia* is represented above all in the story of the Cyclops, who traps, kills, and eats his guests. He even distorts the custom by offering a perverse guest-gift to Odysseus: he will kill and eat the hero last of all the captive Greeks.[37]

Euripides adopts the theme of the guest-host relationship from Homer's story of Polyphemus and Odysseus, using the terms *xenos* (guest/host) and *xenia* (guest-host relationship) twenty-three times in the short play. In addition, Odysseus asks if the Sicilians are 'lovers of strangers' (*philoxenoi*, 125), Polyphemus is twice called a 'guest-eater' (*xenodaitumos*, 610 and *xenodaita*, 658), and Sicily is dubbed 'unfriendly to guests' (*axenon*, 91). These examples amount to about one mention of guests, hosts, or the guest-host relationship every twenty-six lines, an average that confirms the thematic importance of *xenia* in the play. And Euripides employs the theme fairly predictably. When Polyphemus walks onstage, for example, he is clearly unaware of or indifferent to the Greek cultural custom of reciprocal hospitality. His only concern is to find out whether or not the strangers who have appeared at his cave are pirates, and he observes none of the expected, appropriate rules of engagement. Instead, he immediately asks the men who they are, where they sailed from, and what city 'educated' them (275–6). Similarly—although from the opposite point of view—Odysseus pleads for his men's lives by focusing directly on *xenia*, saying (299–301), 'it is a custom for mortals to receive shipwrecked men from the sea and to give gifts of hospitality'.

Homer's interest in the guest-host relationship results in a certain contrast between the cultured Greek and the barbaric foreigner, a juxtaposition that can also be seen in Euripides' *Cyclops*.[38] The Cyclopes who dwell in Sicily are solitary monsters who live in caves with no cities or government, and they eat only meat, cheese, and milk, and never cultivate the land.[39] The solitary life and lack of government would have been viewed as particularly uncultured by the Athenians. Odysseus, on the other hand, in his repeated questions to Silenus near the start of the play establishes himself as a cultured, modern-day Athenian who expects Greek civilization to have influenced the inhabitants of Sicily. He even asks whether the Cyclopes' island is ruled by the people (119), a clear reference to Athens' democratic system of government. But throughout the rest of the play, Euripides does not treat the theme of 'civilized vs. uncivilized' in such a clear-cut manner as the Homeric original. Instead, he complicates the model by making Polyphemus a more sophisticated figure than the Homeric prototype and making Odysseus somewhat more barbaric.

Although Polyphemus is an uncivilized, un-Greek monster, Euripides infuses his character with some distinctly cultured qualities.[40] For example, in the *Odyssey*, when Polyphemus discovers Odysseus and the other Greeks in his cave, he immediately smashes two of the men on the rocks and consumes them without cooking them. In Euripides' version, however, Polyphemus orders that the flesh be prepared very carefully:

Κυ.　οὔκουν κοπίδας ὡς τάχιστ' ἰὼν
　　　θήξεις μαχαίρας καὶ μέγαν φάκελον ξύλων
　　　ἐπιθεὶς ἀνάψεις; ὡς σφαγέντες αὐτίκα
　　　πλήσουσι νηδὺν τὴν ἐμὴν ἀπ' ἄνθρακος
　　　θερμὴν διδόντες δαῖτα τῷ κρεανόμῳ
　　　τὰ δ' ἐκ λέβητος ἐφθὰ καὶ τετηκότα.

Euripides' Cyclops 241–6

Cyc:　Go sharpen the cleaving knives as quickly as possible
　　　and lay down a big bundle of wood for me,
　　　then fire it up. As soon as I slaughter them
　　　and pull them from the coals, they will fill my belly,
　　　supplying a warm meal to the meat carver,
　　　and the rest will be stewed and softened in the cauldron.

Rather than eating like a wild beast, Polyphemus wants to create an enjoyable and carefully prepared feast for himself. He focuses on cooking methods and devices, and Odysseus' account of Polyphemus' feast (382–404) similarly highlights the monster's fascination with culinary details.[41]

Euripides' portrayal of a more sophisticated Cyclops complicates the Homeric model, and this can also be seen in his similarly less clear-cut and more barbaric version of Odysseus. In Homer's *Odyssey*, the island of the Cyclopes grows grapes, and Polyphemus drinks wine unmixed, which demonstrates a lack of culture and refinement.[42] In Euripides' version, however, there are no grapes or wine (or Dionysus) on the island. Polyphemus' ignorance of wine and the god almost lends a sympathetic quality to the monster, since it is not merely that he is disrespectful to Dionysus, as Pentheus is in Euripides' *Bacchae*, but he is unfamiliar with the god and his power.[43] When he is exposed to the wine and thereby symbolically initiated into the Dionysian *thiasos*, he actually wants to behave appropriately by sharing the god with the other Cyclopes. Since Euripides' version of the myth has no giant boulder blocking the doorway of the cave, Odysseus and his companions could easily have given Polyphemus enough wine to pass out and then simply walked out of the cave, back to their ship.[44] There was no need to stab out Polyphemus' eye at all. For Odysseus and probably for the Athenian audience, the monster could never redeem himself or escape revenge after the heinous consumption of Odysseus' men, but these adaptations show how Euripides manipulates the myth to bring hero and monster a little closer together, with a less stark distinction between Polyphemus' barbarism and Odysseus' civility.

Euripides presents similarly complex versions of the protagonist and antagonist in Odysseus' and Polyphemus' philosophical positions. Odysseus repeatedly and vigorously questions the power of the gods, and although Polyphemus admits that the gods exist, he openly disparages them and their temples, belittling Zeus and his thunderbolts in particular. Both characters' sentiments represent actual contemporary arguments that were seen by many in Athens as influential and troubling ideas propagated by sophistic agitators.[45] Euripides offers a particularly interesting connection between Polyphemus and the fifth-century Athenian political philosopher

Callicles as he is represented in Plato's *Gorgias*.[46] Polyphemus' philosophical/sophistic tendencies appear above all in verses 315–46, where the giant extols wealth, disparages laws and customs, and suggests that the gods have little impact on our existence, so long as we are able to enjoy life. He contends that there is only one god worthy of reverence: wealth. He also states that he will make sacrifices to no deity other than his own stomach.[47] Zeus can send rain, snow, thunder, and lightning, but Polyphemus has a warm cave, animal skins, and plenty of food and drink, so the god cannot harm him.

Polyphemus' concept of power is bound up in satisfying his appetites, even if it means offending laws, customs, and the gods. He clearly suggests that the most powerful being, whether man or monster, has the right to enjoy whatever he wishes, a concept remarkably similar to Callicles' theory in Plato's *Gorgias*:

> Natural decency and justice ... demand that the person who would live properly should allow his appetites to grow as powerful as possible and should not check them, should serve them when they are at their height through manliness and intelligence and should satisfy his appetites as they arise.
>
> Plato, *Gorgias* 491e6–492a2, trans. Hunter 2009, 68

Callicles stresses that those who 'would live properly' should have rights over the weak and that when someone gains power, he must have overlapping conceptions of *nomoi* (customs/laws) with those who are weak. But even so, those who are strong should always have authority. The Cyclops and Plato's Callicles are adamant that one's appetites should not be curbed and that powerful people have the right to satisfy their desires.

Polyphemus and Callicles also have similar positions on wealth and hedonism. Polyphemus (317) says that material goods are the only things that matter to those who are wise, dismissing everything else (such as customs and laws, *nomoi*), as 'noise and nice-sounding words'. Callicles makes more or less the same philosophical points in the *Gorgias*:

Expensive pleasures and unrestrained behavior and freedom, this is virtue and happiness, if they have support. All of these embellishments, namely the agreements which men make contrary to nature, are worthless nonsense.

Plato, *Gorgias* 492c4–7, trans. Hunter 2009, 69

Callicles' sentiment is functionally very similar to Polyphemus' ideas that laws which infringe on mankind's pleasures are mere complications to human life. The Cyclops further presents these sophistic ideas when he equates wealth with pleasure and hedonism:

ὡς τοὐμπιεῖν γε καὶ φαγεῖν τοὐφ' ἡμέραν,
Ζεὺς οὗτος ἀνθρώποισι τοῖσι σώφροσιν,
λυπεῖν δὲ μηδὲν αὐτόν. οἳ δὲ τοὺς νόμους
ἔθεντο ποικίλλοντες ἀνθρώπων βίον,
κλαίειν ἄνωγα·

Euripides *Cyclops* 336–40

To eat and drink every day,
this is Zeus for men of sound mind—
this and the avoidance of grief. Those who established
laws and complicated the life of men
can go to hell.

Euripides forms the monster in the image of an uncivilized, pre-civilized brute, but also a sophisticated contemporary Athenian thinker. From a pre-civilized point of view, Polyphemus' philosophy makes a great deal of sense: all he should be concerned with is the daily need for food and drink. From a post-civilized point of view, Polyphemus' philosophy engages with the Calliclean concept that laws are a waste of time and that power is supreme. For both the Cyclops and the philosopher, natural law should rule the world.[48] As Hunter points out, this means that Polyphemus, 'far from being a "savage", has in fact passed beyond the constraints of "civilisation", and Cyclops society may thus be thought of as both pre- and post- the rule of νόμος'.[49]

The parallels between Polyphemus and Callicles suggest that Euripides engaged with sophists and sophistic philosophy in the *Cyclops*.[50] Even the character of Odysseus, who generally represents the civilized world, is a more complex character than the Homeric exemplar. Odysseus is ostensibly represented as a proponent of civilization in Euripides' play, just as Polyphemus is superficially the 'uncivilized' monster. The Greek hero repeatedly attempts to appeal to Polyphemus' sense of culture, as in the following verses:[51]

... ἀλλ' ἐμοὶ πιθοῦ, Κύκλωψ·
πάρες τὸ μάργον σῆς γνάθου, τὸ δ' εὐσεβὲς
τῆς δυσσεβείας ἀνθελοῦ· πολλοῖσι γὰρ
κέρδη πονηρὰ ζημίαν ἠμείψατο.

Euripides, Cyclops 309–12

But listen to me, Cyclops,
forget about your gluttonous jaw and choose piety
over impiety; for improper profit
has brought in its wake downfall for many people.

These lines offer a standard Odyssean, civilized retort to Polyphemus' actions, but elsewhere Odysseus presents more contentious contemporary ideas, especially in his treatment of the gods. For example, Zeus is unexpectedly missing from Odysseus' account of how the hero and his men ended up on the island of the Cyclopes. In the *Odyssey*, the ship is driven off course by winds sent by the king of the gods, but in Euripides' version, the weather alone is the cause.[52] By removing Zeus from the plot, Euripides reflects contemporary, scientific discussion on natural phenomena and inherently questions the power of the gods.[53]

Odysseus also addresses the role of the gods in the lives of humans when he is faced with hopeless destruction at the hand of the Cyclops. Like Polyphemus, the hero has doubts about the rule of Zeus:

σύ τ', ὦ φαεννὰς ἀστέρων οἰκῶν ἕδρας
Ζεῦ ξένι', ὅρα τάδ'· εἰ γὰρ αὐτὰ μὴ βλέπεις,
ἄλλως νομίζῃ Ζεὺς τὸ μηδὲν ὢν θεός.

Euripides Cyclops 353–5

And you, oh Zeus Xenia, who inhabits the shining
seats of the stars, look upon these things. For if you do not see
    them,
you are wrongly thought to be divine Zeus, when actually you are
    nothing at all.

Odysseus repeats this sentiment again at 606–7, when he says that
if the gods do not save him and his men from dying, then 'we must
consider Chance a god, and the gods subservient to Chance'. This is
a powerful shift from Homer's *Odyssey*, where the fickleness of the
gods is par for the course.[54] Odysseus suggests that Zeus is beholden
to the constraints that the god has established regarding *xenia*. In the
Homeric epics, however, there are no such guarantees—there is little
predictability of divine action in accord with any particular standards.[55]

The gods' actions in Homer's world are based on chance, not on
human expectations of the gods' actions, but the capricious gods
are replaced in Euripides' *Cyclops*, and they are doubted by both
Polyphemus and Odysseus. There is, though, one god in the play who
does not suffer any negative comments or depictions, Dionysus. In fact,
unlike in Homer's *Odyssey*, where Odysseus comes up with his own plan
to defeat Polyphemus (9.318), in Euripides' *Cyclops* Odysseus receives
a divine idea (v. 411), presumably because Dionysus has inspired the
hero to use wine to defeat the monster.[56] In addition to portraying the
god in a positive light, Euripides seems to update Dionysus, using the
name Bromios more than any other appellation, a designation that
does not appear in epic and is decidedly 'newer'.[57] The mythological
world that Euripides explores here has evolved from Homer's *Odyssey*.
The exploration of *xenia* remains, but the juxtaposition of civilized and
uncivilized is less clear, with Polyphemus and Odysseus being more

complex characters who engage in the cultural and philosophical debates of contemporary Athens. Euripides' Polyphemus is a gourmand and a philosopher, and his Odysseus is a cynical agnostic who insists on killing the Cyclops even though it is unnecessary.

Sicilian expedition

Although Euripides engages with themes drawn directly from Homer's *Odyssey* and historically significant religious Dionysiac themes, he also represents the time and place in which he was writing.[58] He creates more multifaceted, 'contemporary' versions of Polyphemus and Odysseus. He also appears to update the myth in a way that alludes to recent historical events, particularly the infamous Sicilian Expedition. From 415 to 413, the Athenians waged a battle to incorporate Sicily into their 'Empire'.[59] Although they lacked structure and focus at the start of the expedition, they had success until the Spartans roused the local Sicilians and organized a counter-attack. The Athenians lost a number of battles on land and sea and ultimately were defeated, with the loss of around two hundred ships and thousands of soldiers.[60]

As Plutarch notes, many of the Athenians who were caught after the defeat were held prisoner in Sicilian rock quarries with very little food and water, while others were secreted away, branded on their foreheads, and sold as slaves.[61] Some, though, are reputed to have been saved because they could quote the plays of Euripides, whose poetry was revered above all others in Sicily.[62] Plutarch's account provides remarkable anecdotal evidence for the fame of Euripides throughout the Greek world, but it also offers a glimpse at the terrible fate suffered by a number of Athenian soldiers. It is a grim vision of what the Athenians must have been reflecting on after their terrible defeat in Sicily. The Athenian population, especially the population of soldiers, had been reduced significantly, and few, if any, families would have escaped the expedition without the loss of loved ones. The Athenians were quick to rebuild their fleet, but the financial cost damaged their economy, and from a historical perspective, the loss in Sicily is typically considered the turning point in the Peloponnesian War, the event that led to the ultimate defeat of the Athenians.[63]

Euripides seems to have composed his satyr play with this painful loss in mind. As Thucydides (6.2.1) notes in his *History of the Peloponnesian War*, the Athenians considered the earliest inhabitants of Sicily to be the Cyclopes, a connection that Euripides seems to draw upon in updating his *Cyclops* for Athens.[64] Not only has Euripides moved the action of the play from the geographically uncertain Homeric world to the island of Sicily, but he also mentions Sicily and Mt. Aetna a remarkable thirteen times over the course of the play. Euripides repeatedly disconnects the play from the mythological setting and connects it with the location of Athens' recent military defeat.[65] This association establishes the fifth-century inhabitants of Sicily (i.e. the people who just defeated the Athenians) as the descendants of the Cyclopes, a powerful correlation for the audience. The Athenian Expedition maps onto the story of Odysseus and Polyphemus in other ways as well. Thucydides notes (6.1.1) that the Athenians did not realize the size of Sicily or the number of its inhabitants.[66] Nor did they realize that such a simple expedition would have such severe consequences. Like the Athenians of the Sicilian Expedition, the overly proud Greek hero, Odysseus, sails to a land he does not fully understand and is unprepared for the ensuing encounter with the locals. Then, before he is able to flee, he suffers the loss of some of his comrades and ensures for himself a devastating punishment at sea, where nearly everyone will be lost.[67] Euripides may even have drawn on this myth because the audience would have been mindful of the poet's role in saving Athenian soldiers who were captured by barbarians and confined to a rocky prison. Polyphemus and the Cyclopes represent the Sicilian natives; Odysseus and his men are the arrogant and ill-prepared Athenians; Polyphemus' cave is the rock quarry that imprisons the Greeks; and Euripides' poetry literally saves the day, with the prisoners escaping through the poet's theatrical creation.

Conclusion

As we have seen, Euripides incorporates a number of relevant contemporary issues in the *Cyclops*. He places Athenian Dionysiac ritual in a prominent position throughout the play, mentioning Dionysus and Dionysian religious elements repeatedly. He also employs metatheatrical self-awareness throughout the performance, with Silenus, Polyphemus, and the chorus of satyrs drawing attention to the production as a play. In all of these instances, Euripides connects the production to the god of the theatre, repeatedly showing that his *Cyclops* has 'Something to do with Dionysus'. But Euripides also connects traditionally Homeric thematic elements to contemporary Athens, especially in the examination of Polyphemus and Odysseus as representatives of the civilized and uncivilized worlds. Euripides complicates Homer's Polyphemus by making him an uncivilized brute with fifth-century interests in philosophy and gastronomy. Euripides' Odysseus is similarly complex. He is a proponent of the gods and customs, but is somewhat barbaric in his unnecessary stabbing of Polyphemus, and like the Cyclops, he too presents certain fifth-century sophistic ideas that were condemned by Athenians. The play even associates Odysseus and the Athenians in a not particularly flattering manner through connections to the recent Athenian Expedition in Sicily. Euripides does not just 'Take one myth, add satyrs, observe result.'[68] Despite staying quite close to the Homeric original, he updates the story, filling his play with allusions to contemporary religion, performance, philosophy, and history.

4

Euripides' *Cyclops* in Its Literary Context

When examining the literary history of Athenian drama, we tend to concentrate (often by necessity) on the reception of a particular work. Greek drama has had a substantial influence on Western civilization. Through various periods, places, and modes of presentation, ancient Greek plays have served as models for artists to explore their own cultures.[1] Seneca revised Greek tragedies to suit Rome under Emperor Nero, Handel composed his *Hercules* as an eighteenth-century operatic version of Sophocles' *Women of Trachis*, Wole Soyinka rewrote Euripides' *Bacchae* to explore the civil unrest in post-colonial Nigeria, and Spike Lee adapted Aristophanes' *Lysistrata* to examine inner-city gun violence in Chicago with his 2015 film *Chi-Rac*. Euripides' *Cyclops*, however, presents a unique example in the history of Athenian theatrical productions. Unlike the majority of surviving ancient Greek plays, the literary exemplar from which the plot was derived is both extant and much more famous than the play itself.[2] The Homeric predecessor of the *Cyclops*, book nine of Homer's *Odyssey*, is one of the most famous scenes in all Greek literature and, as such, it significantly overshadows the *Cyclops* in the history of the myth's reception. In fact, there is little, if anything, that can be ascribed strictly to the influence of Euripides' play.[3] Nevertheless, Euripides' *Cyclops* has a fascinating historical relationship with earlier literary works and genres. As we will see in this chapter, these relationships appear to be informed above all by the connection Euripides establishes between satyr drama and comedy. This comic connection not only influences the humour of the *Cyclops*, but shapes its interaction with various predecessors. Euripides uses contemporary comic techniques to outshine previous authors of satyr plays and even to rewrite and surpass Homer, as he alludes to and engages with a variety of archaic and classical works, including epic, hymns, comedies, and tragedies.

Satyr play, *kômos*-song

As we saw in the previous chapter, Euripides repeatedly uses the term *kômos* (revelry) in performative and religious contexts throughout the *Cyclops* and uses it infrequently in his tragedies, a fact that draws special attention to satyr drama's historical connections to Dionysiac *kômos*-song. But *kômos*-song also has a significant relationship with Greek comedy, a fact that persisted in *kômôidia*'s etymology as 'revelry song': *kômos* (revelry, merrymaking) and *ôidê/aoidê* (song). Comedy and satyr drama's associations with *kômos*-song created a literary-historical connection between the two genres based on their mutual development out of some of the same pre-theatrical precursors.[4] Evidence for this generic connection can be seen in a number of archaic sources, but it also persisted into later periods. Plato, Aristotle, Demetrius, and various satyr vases present important generic connections between comedy and satyr play.[5] Euripides' *Cyclops* and *Alcestis* show that even Euripides appears to have written satyr drama with this particular historical relationship in mind.

Ancient Greek comedy was officially established at the City Dionysia in 486, and satyr drama was incorporated a decade or two earlier, but comic and satyric performances predate both genres.[6] These performances were related to and evolved from dithyrambic *kômos* (revelry) song.[7] The early history of dithyramb is impossible to reconstruct with confidence, but one thing that is reasonably clear is its connection to *kômos*-song, since it was referred to as *kômos* in inscriptional and literary evidence.[8] Etymology offers a clear connection between dithyramb (i.e. *kômos*-song) and comedy, but the associations between dithyramb and satyric performance in archaic Greece are equally compelling. A number of vases depict both satyrs and komasts (practitioners of the *kômos*) as companions of Dionysus in mythological representations and performance, especially the popular 'Return of Hephaestus'.[9] Satyrs and komasts are also similarly partial to sex, wine, dance, and song. And there are a number of Athenian vases (mostly from the later fifth century), on which satyrs are labelled with the name 'Komos'.[10] In addition, ancient legend connects dithyramb and satyr play through Arion of Methymna, who was said to be the inventor of dithyramb and the first person to introduce satyrs to speaking roles.[11] Satyric and komastic figures can even be found on the same vases and in the same contexts, as on the Corinthian alabastron in Figure 4.1, where the artist blends komast and satyr in a single figure.[12] As these vases, inscriptions, and anecdotes suggest, satyr drama and comedy developed together out of and alongside dithyramb.

Aristotle too suggests a potential connection between satyr drama and comedy's early development from dithyramb. Although he maintains that dithyramb was tragedy's precursor (*Poetics* 1449a, 10–11) and phallic songs were comedy's precursor (1449a, 12–14), he also states that tragedy evolved out of something 'satyr-drama-like'.[13] This inherently connects dithyramb with satyric performance, but the phallic songs performed by satyrs also connect satyric performance with the phallic productions of comedy. Nagy presents a helpful synopsis of Aristotle's generic theory (2007, 123):

> Aristotle is positing here an early phase of drama where proto-tragedy and proto-comedy are already differentiated, but these prototypes are seen as forms that have not yet reached the ultimate forms of tragedy and comedy, because tragedy has not yet been differentiated from dithyramb, whereas the satyr drama has not yet been differentiated from comedy. By implication, there is a still earlier phase where tragedy/ dithyramb are not yet differentiated from satyr drama/comedy.

Figure 4.1 Corinthian-style Boeotian black-figure alabastron, *c*. 575–550 BCE. Göttingen, Archäologisches Institut der Universität HU 533g. Photo: Stephan Eckardt.

Aristotle thus presents a complicated blueprint for the history of the theatre, where satyric performances are related to tragedy because both had dithyrambic associations, but they were also related to comedy because both were phallic songs. Before comic and satyric performances were full-fledged theatrical genres, they were less differentiated *kômos*-songs, emerging out of the same dithyrambic choral revels. Comedy developed out of *kômos*-song, but so too did satyr drama, since satyrs were Dionysus' main troop of komasts.

Although the relationship between comedy and satyr drama developed even before the genres existed, when they were pre-comic and pre-satyric performances, the generic associations continued for centuries.[14] It seems that Euripides even addressed the generic relationship in his *Cyclops* and his *Alcestis*, the latter of which was a production staged in place of a satyr play but without a chorus of satyrs. His frequent use of *kômos* in both of these plays appears not only to have served as a reference to Dionysiac religion, ritual, and performance, but it also served to associate satyr play with comedy as *kômos*-song. Euripides dramatizes Homer's famous tale of Odysseus and the Cyclops with a number of humorous flourishes, but more importantly, he uses the play's generic associations with comedy to establish the *Cyclops* as a vehicle for comedic literary criticism.

Part of satyr drama's meaning was no doubt bound up in the comedy-like laughter that it evoked at the City Dionysia.[15] Satyr plays contained a number of humorous elements, most of which grew from Silenus and the chorus of satyrs. The satyrs' stage phallus provides perhaps the most notable connection to comedy, with both genres employing a costume phallus as part of their generic identity. In fact, most of the *Cyclops*' jokes focus on the phallus. For example, at the start of the play, Silenus laments the labours he is enduring as the servant of Polyphemus; they are, he says, even worse than the labours he suffered in his youth, when his flesh was strong. As Seaford has noted, δέμας (flesh) is likely a sexual reference to Silenus' flaccid costume phallus,[16] an allusion that is underscored by Silenus' repeated use of the phallic word δόρυ (spear) throughout the remainder of the monologue.[17] The humorous repetition of phallic vocabulary would have been further emphasized in performance by Silenus' onstage actions, as he grabbed his costume phallus to imitate these actions. Silenus presents similarly sexual language and action in his encomium to wine:

ἵν' ἔστι τουτί τ' ὀρθὸν ἐξανιστάναι
μαστοῦ τε δραγμὸς καὶ παρεσκευασμένον
ψαῦσαι χεροῖν λειμῶνος ...

Euripides, Cyclops 169–70

[Drinking] is where you get this thing to stand up straight,
where you can grab a breast and get prepared
to run your hands through a woman's 'bush'.

In these sexually charged verses Silenus indicates that a sip of wine will both give him an erection and excite him to seek out a female companion. His use of the technical term μαστοῦ (breast) is explicitly sexual and his use of λειμῶνος (moist, grassy meadow) is a metaphorical allusion to the mons pubis.[18] Silenus also employs the demonstrative adjective τουτί to refer to his penis, which shows that he must have made some gesture towards the attached costume phallus, perhaps by pointing towards it or grabbing it.[19]

Much like their father, the satyrs offer sexual jests that focus on their penises, as in verses 177–81, where the satyrs ask Odysseus about his exploits in Troy:

Χο. ἐλάβετε Τροίαν τὴν Ἑλένην τε χειρίαν;
Οδ. καὶ πάντα γ' οἶκον Πριαμιδῶν ἐπέρσαμεν.
Χο. οὔκουν, ἐπειδὴ τὴν νεᾶνιν εἵλετε,
    ἅπαντες αὐτὴν διεκροτήσατ' ἐν μέρει,
    ἐπεί γε πολλοῖς ἥδεται γαμουμένη

Euripides, Cyclops 177–81

Chor: Did you take into your hands both Troy and Helen?

Odys: Yes, and we sacked the whole house of the sons of Priam.
Chor: So, when you caught the young woman,
        did you all take turns pounding her,
        since she enjoys being 'married' to multiple men?

Obviously, the satyrs intend something sexual when they ask Odysseus if he got Helen in his hands, but Odysseus interprets the question figuratively. The satyrs follow with another ambiguous question: did the whole Greek army 'pound her/pierce her through?' Here, the satyrs employ militaristic language to imply having sex with Helen and then complete the thought with a euphemistic use of γαμέω, which can mean both to marry and to have intercourse.[20] Later in the play they address the disuse of their phalluses (439–40), saying that for a long time their 'dear siphon has been widowed'. The term σίφων, which traditionally denotes a 'siphon, used for drawing wine out of a cask or jar', refers to the satyrs' *phalloi* in this instance. Euripides draws on an interesting connection between the satyrs' desire for sex and wine, and here the phallic shape of the siphon and the satyrs' costume phallus would have made the connections entirely literal: the satyrs call their 'siphons' widowed because they have not been used for so long.[21]

Although the *Cyclops* presents a range of jokes, its humour alone does not necessarily ensure a relation to comedy. The *Cyclops'* jokes and its focus on the phallus suggest a comic-generic connection, but they do not alone support the idea that Euripides constructed his satyr play with comedy in mind. The numerous uses of κῶμος in the *Cyclops* also suggest a conscious connection between comedy and satyr drama, since satyr drama and comedy were both *kômos*-songs. But we find our greatest evidence that Euripides associated these two genres in the *Alcestis*, which is, after the *Cyclops* and perhaps Sophocles' *Ichneutae*, our most important literary evidence for ancient satyr drama, even though it has no satyrs.

In 438, Euripides staged three tragedies at the City Dionysia (*Cretan Women, Alcmaeon in Psophis,* and *Telephus*), and he concluded his tetralogy not with a satyr play, but with the satyr-less *Alcestis*.[22] Although some scholars believe that this play was not the only satyr-less satyr play (there is no evidence to support this theory), the most compelling explanation for Euripides' choice to stage the *Alcestis* is related to legislation that limited comedy from around 440–436:[23]

ἐπ' Εὐθυμένους ἄρχοντος—οὗτός ἐστιν ὁ ἄρχων, ἐφ' οὗ κατελύθη τὸ ψήφισμα τὸ περὶ τοῦ μὴ κωμῳδεῖν γραφὲν ἐπὶ Μορυχίδου [440/39]. ἴσχυσε δὲ ἐκεῖνόν τε τὸν ἐνιαυτὸν καὶ τοὺς δύο ἑξῆς ἐπι Γλαυκίνου [439/8] τε καὶ Θεοδώρου [438/7], μεθ' οὓς Εὐθυμένου [437/6] κατελύθη.

In the archonship of Euthymenes: this is the archon in whose term was dissolved the law against ridiculing, which was passed in the archonship of Morychides (440/39). It was in force during that year and the two years following in the archonships of Glaukinos (439/8) and Theodoros (438/7), after which it was dissolved in the archonship of Euthymenes.

Trans. Csapo and Slater (1995, 176)

The so-called Decree of Morychides appears to have prohibited 'making comedy' (μὴ κωμῳδεῖν), but as we know from various testimonia, comedy continued to be performed in Athens during this time.[24] The law was not actually meant to ban comedy, but to ban Old Comedy's most prominent feature, *onomasti kômôidein*, 'making fun of people by name'.

Although the intention of the Decree of Morychides would have been clear to Athenians, Euripides appears to have interpreted the imprecise language of the law literally and, therefore, humorously, or even ironically. Satyr drama, as a genre of mythological plots that did not make fun of people by name (at this point in its history at least[25]), was not implicated in the law, but Euripides linked satyr drama with comedy through their mutual association to *kômos*-song. He comments on the law by removing the satyrs and repeatedly using *kômos* (and related terms) throughout the *Alcestis*. In the play, Alcestis' husband Admetus bans revelry (*kômos*), just as *kômôidein* (making comedy) had been banned in Athens by the Decree of Morychides.[26] Euripides juxtaposes the laughter and partying of the past with the wailing of the present, a metaphor that maps perfectly onto the historical events at the City Dionysia: if *kômos*-song (comedy) is prohibited, then satyr drama and the raucous actions of the satyrs are prohibited, and what remains is the tragic *Alcestis*. By drawing attention to the relationship between comedy and satyr drama in this play, Euripides influenced comedy and satyr vases for decades. Comic poets started immediately and vigorously using satyrs in their comedies, and ancient vase painters merged satyrs, *kômos*-song, and *kômôidia* in a number of ways.[27]

Euripides' association of satyr drama and comedy in the *Alcestis* suggests that his repeated use of *kômos* in the *Cyclops* was also a meaningful choice, with similar implications about the play's generic connections to comedy. Satyr drama relates to comic drama in humour, use of the phallus, and a mutual historical connection to *kômos*-song, but perhaps the association most important for understanding the *Cyclops* is Euripides' comedic approach to his play's predecessors. It is a trope in Greek Old Comedy for the author to establish himself as the best comic playwright (often using metatheatrical language), and it is also common for him to connect his work with other genres and authors of the Greek literary tradition; then he establishes himself and his work as superior even to them, as he engages in a non-scholastic version of competitive literary criticism.[28] Aristophanes, for example, frequently argues that he is a better comic poet than his rivals in comedy, but he also repeatedly alludes to, comments on, and rewrites Euripides' tragedies in a way that suggests he is better even than poets outside the tradition of comedy.[29]

Euripides engages in a similar, though less overt, version of literary criticism and one-upmanship in the *Cyclops*, presenting a play teeming with performative language and literary references.[30] As we saw in the previous chapter, Euripides uses formal theatrical and religious-performative language throughout the play (e.g. *sikinnis*, chorus, *kômos*), but he also establishes himself as a superior poet of satyr plays. In the prologue, Silenus laments his 'countless troubles' as a servant and companion of the god Dionysus, but being stranded on the island of the Cyclopes as a slave to Polyphemus is, he notes, the greatest of all his trials (v. 10). On the face of it, this is typical satyric posturing. In fact, Silenus cannot believe these labours himself, asking in the middle of his rant on fighting in the Gigantomachy, if he dreamed everything (v. 8). However, this prologue also offers a clever meta-literary reference to the genre of satyr drama and praise for the *Cyclops* and its author. By mentioning his innumerable past experiences, Silenus playfully alludes to the innumerable satyr plays performed on this very stage, since the main vehicle for all of his mythological experiences was satyr drama at the City Dionysia. In Greek mythological history, Silenus did not take part in the Gigantomachy, Hera's maddening of Dionysus, or the story of the Tyrrhenian pirates, just as he had not taken part in Odysseus' encounter with Polyphemus. But Euripides exploits the repetitive nature of satyr drama by alluding to *topoi* that were (or could be) associated with satyr plays. Silenus' use of 'countless troubles' functions to transform myths in which Silenus took no part into plots of earlier satyr plays in which he did take part.

By the time the *Cyclops* was staged, there had been hundreds of satyr plays performed at the City Dionysia, and satyr drama was in constant dialogue with itself. Silenus' prologue signals that he, his sons, and the audience have been here before. And Silenus' reference to the myths of earlier satyr plays, along with his insistence that this particular plot surpasses them all, functions as a clever sort of literary criticism, since it suggests that this play surpasses all other satyr plays.[31] Euripides uses the repetitive nature of satyr drama to establish himself as the best tragedian/satyr dramatist, past or present. He then returns to this perpetual intra-generic relationship at the end of the play, when the satyrs note that they will be the slaves of Dionysus for all time. In addition to the important religious overtones of these verses, the final choral couplet implies that the satyrs will sometime soon return to the stage, either as slaves of Dionysus or of some ogre-ish figure. Whether willing slaves or unwilling slaves, the satyrs will always be freed from one form of slavery and return to the other. Then, at the end of every satyr play, they will be ready to restart their journey with the next playwright or at next year's festival.[32]

Homer's *Odyssey*

In the *Cyclops*, Euripides uses meta-performative language and the constant connection and interchange between satyr plays to present a complex and competitive literary relationship with other authors of satyr drama. He presents a similar literary relationship with his Homeric source material. Euripides clearly knew Homer's version of the *Odyssey* quite well and draws amply upon that knowledge, although the language of the play makes it seem unlikely that he was constantly consulting the text while composing his play.[33] There are a few apparent intertexts, but on the whole the *Cyclops* goes beyond translating Homer for the stage.[34] Instead, it functions more as a form of early literary criticism than of straightforward imitation.[35] In the previous section, we saw that Silenus and the satyrs seem to be aware that they are in a satyr play, but they (and the other characters) seem also to be aware that they are in a theatrical version of Homer's *Odyssey*. They know the Homeric epic that formed their script, and they know that the audience knows the model as well. Euripides frequently draws attention to everyone's knowledge of the exemplar by making pointed, playful associations that are more literary game and mythic-literary criticism than an attempt to faithfully reproduce Homer onstage.

As we have seen, Euripides actively acknowledges that the *Cyclops* is a reiteration of the constantly reiterated genre of satyr drama at the start of the play with Silenus' 'countless troubles' (v. 1), but these countless troubles also relate to Odysseus' legendary 'many pains' (πολλὰ ἄλγεα) at the start of Homer's *Odyssey* (1.4).[36] Euripides begins his play about Odysseus with a reference to one of the most famous line of the *Odyssey*. Silenus' allusion to Homer's Odysseus puts the elderly satyr in the tradition of great Greek heroes and emphasizes his knowledge of Homer's *Odyssey*. Silenus then reasserts his familiarity with the epic poem when he first meets Odysseus:

Σι. χαῖρ᾽, ὦ ξέν᾽, ὅστις δ᾽ εἶ φράσον πάτραν τε σήν.
Οδ. Ἴθακος Ὀδυσσεύς, γῆς Κεφαλλήνων ἄναξ.
Σι. οἶδ᾽ ἄνδρα, κρόταλον δριμύ, Σισύφου γένος.

Euripides, Cyclops 102–4

> Silenus: Greetings, stranger, tell me who you are and where you're from.
> Odysseus: I am Ithacan Odysseus, lord of the land of Cephallene.
> Silenus: I know the man, the clever chatterer, offspring of Sisyphus.

At first glance, this appears to be a straightforward joke aimed at the hero Odysseus, but the joke turns out to be a playful literary reference. By saying that Silenus already knows Odysseus, it suggests that he is familiar with the Odyssean myth, but it also toys with the Homeric model. Directly after acknowledging his familiarity with the *Odyssey*, he flouts that knowledge, by offering an alternate mythology of Odysseus' parentage, in which his mother was impregnated by Sisyphus before she wed his father. Silenus parodically rewrites Homer, but he adds another level to the literary reference by directly alluding to the first line of the *Odyssey*: ἄνδρα μοι ἔννεπε, Μοῦσα, πολύτροπον … (Sing, O Muse, of the man of many ways). Silenus could have used the second person address to Odysseus, saying, 'I know you' or 'I've heard of you', but instead uses the more bizarre third person, 'I know the man.' By saying that he knows the first word, the titular word, of the *Odyssey* (ἄνδρα), Silenus indicates that he is familiar not only with the hero but also with Homer's epic story of the hero.

Silenus offers a similarly playful reference when the elderly satyr hears that Odysseus and his men were blown off course while rounding Cape Malea. He draws connections between himself and the hero, saying, 'you've suffered the same fate that I have suffered' (v. 110). There is, though, an inherent irony in Silenus' phrasing. Odysseus has not suffered the same fate as Silenus; the satyr has suffered the same fate as the hero. In fact, Silenus never would have ended up in any of these situations, if Homer had not written them into the *Odyssey*. Silenus seems to realize that the recipe for a satyr play is to 'take one myth, add satyrs, observe result',[37] which results in a constant self-awareness of the mythological fabric from which the plot and the characters were drawn.

Odysseus too highlights his knowledge of the mythological-ness of the story, repeatedly emphasizing the preceding version of himself and working to preserve the Homeric original. For example, he wants to uphold his reputation within the current world that he inhabits, and he seems to worry about the earlier story with which he and everyone else is familiar. When Silenus suggests that Odysseus and his men hide in the cave, he responds:

οὐ δῆτ᾽· ἐπεί τἂν μεγάλα γ᾽ ἡ Τροία στένοι,
εἰ φευξόμεσθ᾽ ἕν᾽ ἄνδρα, μυρίον δ᾽ ὄχλον
Φρυγῶν ὑπέστην πολλάκις σὺν ἀσπίδι.
ἀλλ᾽, εἰ θανεῖν δεῖ, κατθανούμεθ᾽ εὐγενῶς
ἢ ζῶντες αἶνον τὸν πάρος συσσώσομεν.

Euripides *Cyclops* 198–202

Definitely not! Troy would grieve deeply,
if I were to flee a single man. I often fended off
a numberless mob of Phrygians with my shield.
If dying is necessary, I will die nobly;
or if I live, I will preserve my former reputation.

In this passage, Odysseus is not merely lamenting the awful fate of
dying in an unheroic manner. He is also acknowledging his history
as a Homeric, Odyssean hero. His use of *ainos* in particular carries a
double significance. Like every Greek hero, he fears for his reputation,
but he also fears for his 'story/fable'.[38] Odysseus is not just preserving
his heroic status. He is preserving the Homeric myth to which he (and
everyone else) knows he belongs.

Polyphemus too appears to be familiar with Odysseus and his
mythos. After the hero introduces himself as an Ithacan who was
driven off course on his way home from Troy, the Cyclops says:

Κυ.   ἦ τῆς κακίστης οἳ μετήλθεθ' ἁρπαγὰς
      Ἑλένης Σκαμάνδρου γείτον' Ἰλίου πόλιν;
Οδ.   οὗτοι, πόνον τὸν δεινὸν ἐξηντληκότες.
Κυ.   αἰσχρὸν στράτευμά γ', οἵτινες μιᾶς χάριν
      γυναικὸς ἐξεπλεύσατ' ἐς γαῖαν Φρυγῶν.

                                        Euripides, *Cyclops* 280–84

Cy: Are you the ones who went to the city of Ilium,
      which neighbours the Scamander, to snatch that most
      reviled woman, Helen?
Od: We are the ones who endured that terrible labour.
Cy: What a horrible campaign, sailing against the
      land of the Phrygians for the sake of a single woman.

Polyphemus uses traditional language in his critique of the expedition
for Helen,[39] but more importantly, he somehow knows about the
expedition and the critiques of the expedition before Odysseus has
even arrived on his island. Like Euripides' Odysseus, the satyric

Polyphemus realizes that he has been here before, and that he has already learned about Helen and the Trojan War.

Even the most famous element of book nine's plot, the blinding of Polyphemus, gets a playfully mytho-reflexive treatment. The satyr chorus asks Odysseus how he plans to deal with the Cyclops, and they offer a few of their own suggestions (pushing him off a cliff or slitting his throat, 447–8), but Odyssey says he prefers a more tricky strategy. The chorus leader responds by saying that the satyrs have long heard that the hero is clever. Odysseus' cunning is, of course, legendary, and Homer has a few different epithets for the hero in this regard. But the satyrs' knowledge of his cleverness is premature, and the precise language that Euripides uses is significant, since the term *sophos* (clever) is decidedly *not* one of Homer's words. It is a word associated with contemporary Athenian sophistry.[40] Euripides engages with Homer but rejects the formulaic language of archaic epic, updating it for the contemporary audience in a playful way that corresponds to the updated, sophistic philosophical concepts used elsewhere in the play.[41]

Euripides is perhaps at his height of meta-mythological playfulness when Odysseus appears from the cave to describe the horrors of Polyphemus killing and consuming his companions. He says:

Οδ.   ὦ Ζεῦ, τί λέξω, δείν' ἰδὼν ἄντρων ἔσω
κοὐ πιστά, μύθοις εἰκότ' οὐδ' ἔργοις βροτῶν;

Euripides Cyclops 375–6

Od: Oh Zeus, what shall I say, now that I have witnessed these awful, unbelievable things inside the cave, things like tales one might tell, not like the deeds of men?

Odysseus here states that the horrors which took place in the cave are the stuff of stories (*mûthois*), but the term *mûthos* also signifies 'myth', which creates a fascinating and overt reference to the mythological tale found in Homer's *Odyssey*. It is a very self-aware moment in the play, where Odysseus makes clear his knowledge of the story that precedes Euripides' *Cyclops*.[42] Book nine of the *Odyssey* presents a story that has entered the realm of *mûthos* in Greek culture, and to have the star of this myth, Odysseus, openly refer to the plot as a myth is humorously self-conscious and meta-mythological. Euripides squeezes one more playful, mythological joke into this same passage by saying that everything the hero has seen in the cave is *ou pista* (not believable).[43] The primary meaning of this comment is that the horrific events in Polyphemus' cave were incredible or extraordinary. However, Odysseus' phrase can also be interpreted literally, as if to suggest that Odysseus' tale in the *Odyssey* is literally so outrageous that it cannot be believed. The four books in which Odysseus narrates his own story are unique in the *Odyssey*, particularly for their descriptions of implausible monsters and farfetched events, while the rest of the *Odyssey* is largely devoid of supernatural figures and events. Audiences were well aware of the incongruity in Odysseus' tale from the rest of the epic,[44] and Euripides offers the earliest extant literary critique of these stories. He does not, however, write a literary treatise. He presents Homer's story in the familiar theatrical setting at the Athenian festival, in the poetically repetitive and self-conscious genre of satyr play, and he playfully pokes fun at Homer's *Odyssey* by calling it a myth and by overtly describing the events of the myth as beyond belief.

Homeric Hymn to Dionysus

In addition to Homer's *Odyssey*, Euripides also engages with the archaic *Homeric Hymn to Dionysus* (*H.H.* seven), in which the god Dionysus disguises himself as a young man and is abducted by a group of Tyrsenian/Tyrrhenian pirates.[45] The sailors, who assume he is the son of a king, bring him on board their ship, where they attempt to bind him, but the ties keep falling off. The helmsman realizes that the young man must be an Olympian god, and so he begs his fellow sailors to let him go, but the leader scolds him. At this point, Dionysus starts to make strange things happen aboard the ship. Wine runs over the deck, a divine scent develops, a vine with grapes grows from the top of the sail, and ivy twists around the mast with flowers and berries. Frightened, the pirates beg the helmsman to bring the ship to land, but the god transforms himself into a lion and seizes the ship's captain. This leads the other men to jump overboard 'to escape a miserable doom' (v. 51), but the pirates (except for the helmsman, whom the god respects) are turned into dolphins. At the end of the hymn, the poet addresses the god directly in verses that praise Dionysus' role in creating poetry (58-9): 'Hail, child of beautiful Semele! He who forgets you can in no way arrange a sweet song.'

Euripides creatively mashes the plot of the hymn to Dionysus with the story from book nine of Homer's *Odyssey*. As Silenus notes in the prologue, he and his sons were shipwrecked on the island of the Cyclopes when they went to search for Dionysus and the pirates (λῃστῶν, v. 12) who had kidnapped him. The narrative of the Homeric Hymn functions as the impetus for the satyrs' action, which leads them into the Homeric myth of Polyphemus, but Euripides continues to link the archaic myths by making Odysseus and his comrades the very men whom the satyrs seek.[46] When Polyphemus encounters the strangers outside his cave, he uses the same term, 'pirate', as Silenus to identify the Greek heroes:

ἔα· τίν' ὄχλον τόνδ' ὁρῶ πρὸς αὐλίοις;
λῃσταί τινες κατέσχον ἢ κλῶπες χθόνα;

Euripides Cyclops 222-3

Oho! What crowd is this I see near my cave?
Have some pirates or thieves occupied this land?

Odysseus and his men are implicitly the pirates and thieves sought by Silenus and the satyrs, and they even admit to possessing Dionysus, who is represented metonymically by the wine. Odysseus carries around the god, who is trapped in the wineskin. Euripides makes Dionysus the prisoner of the pirate and thief Odysseus, and he even seems to allude to the final verse of the hymn, when Polyphemus becomes the victim of Dionysus. After drinking the Dionysian wine, Polyphemus finally 'knows' the god, but it is not the willing knowledge of friendship and worship. It is the forced knowledge of those who fail to recognize the god. Polyphemus' off-key, out-of-tune song (489–90) reflects this disrespect, since he cannot 'arrange sweet song' (*H.H. to Dionysus*, v. 59). This also explains the enigmatic ending, where the satyrs joyfully march offstage to be eternal servants of Dionysus (708–9), even though they have not actually found the god. Because Odysseus has the wine of Maron, he possesses Dionysus, and the satyrs are not merely leaving behind their predicament on the island of the Cyclopes at the end of the play. They have accomplished their goal of being reunited with their divine master. Euripides has rewritten a traditional myth in a humorous, self-conscious, and comedic manner, making Odysseus and his men the pirates of the Homeric Hymn as he combines two famous stories into a single satyr play.

Epicharmus' and Aristias' *Cyclops*, Cratinus' *Odysseis*, and Callias' *Cyclopes*

Although Euripides merged two archaic models to create the *Cyclops*, he does so in a markedly comical manner, playfully reinterpreting the original myths and providing his own interpretive readings. But he wrote his play in a lengthy tradition of playwrights who had already reinterpreted the myth of Odysseus and Polyphemus for the stage, and he appears to have engaged with them as well. Epicharmus is the earliest poet to have composed a theatrical version of book nine of the *Odyssey*. Various references within Epicharmus' poetry reveal that he was writing comedies during the first quarter of the fifth century, and a number of ancient sources place him in Sicily during the rule of Gelo and Hiero in the 480s and 470s.[47] Aristotle says he is 'much earlier' than the earliest Athenian comic poets, which suggests that he may even have been writing in Sicily during the late sixth century. [48] Chronologically, Aristias of Phlius was second to stage a *Cyclops* and is the earliest known playwright to produce this story in Athens. His play is particularly significant because it was a satyr play, unlike the other three poets in this section, all of whom wrote comedies. Aristias was the son of Pratinas, the supposed inventor of satyr drama, and was regarded as one of the top three authors of satyr play (after Aeschylus and his father).[49] He was staging plays by the 460s, during Euripides' lifetime, but before Euripides actually began presenting his own productions.[50] Cratinus (519–422) and Callias (fl. *c.* 440–430) were contemporary Athenian rivals on the comic stage, and they reworked the myth as *Odysseis* and *Cyclopes* respectively. Although the works of these four authors are so fragmentary that it is impossible to draw much in the way of specific connections to Euripides' *Cyclops*, the popularity of the myth in comic and satyric drama seems to inform Euripides' satyr play, particularly in the interrelated depictions of Polyphemus' feast.

Very little is known about Epicharmus' productions (we do not even know if his plays used a chorus[51]), but we do know that he had a penchant for locating his plays on his home island of Sicily.[52] This presents a potential connection with Euripides' *Cyclops*, since it repeatedly mentions Sicily and its environs (twelve times in seven hundred lines).[53] Although only three verses of Epicharmus' play remain, a more tangible association may be drawn in the similar depiction of the Cyclops as 'a glutton and gourmet'.[54] As we saw in the previous chapter, Homer's *Odyssey* depicts Polyphemus as a barbaric savage, crushing the skulls of Odysseus' men and eating

them whole without cooking them. In Euripides' play, however, the
Cyclops calls for his knife and a fire, and wants some of the meat
roasted and some boiled (241–6). Euripides' depiction of Polyphemus
differs significantly from that found in Homer's *Odyssey*. But a similar
depiction is also evident in Epicharmus' fragments, with Polyphemus
clearly mentioning his mortar at one point and the pleasantness of
the feast at another (K-A 70 and 71). These references, brief though
they are, present a departure from the Homeric original and prefigure
Euripides' interest in Polyphemus as chef.

Euripides and Epicharmus also appear to provide a more developed
drinking scene than is found in Homer. One of Epicharmus'
drinking-themed fragments even uses language similar to that found
in Euripides' *Cyclops*. Epicharmus' Polyphemus says, φέρ' ἐγχέας εἰς
τὸ σκύφος (Epicharmus, K-A 72) (Come on, pour [some wine] into
my cup!). This is comparable to Euripides' version of the drinking
scene, where Polyphemus orders Odysseus, φέρ' ἔγχεόν νυν
(*Cyclops* 566–8) (Come on now and pour). The commands are very
similar, with both Polyphemuses using the imperative φέρε and a
form of ἐγχέω. There is not enough distinctive quality to these verses
to suggest a definite intertext, but the fact that Homer does not use
either of these verbs in the original version presents an intriguing
possibility that Euripides was using Epicharmus' play as a model.

In Athens, Aristias and Cratinus also focused on wine, food, and
the monster's sophisticated gustatory tendencies. Aristias' satyr play
offers little that can be connected to Euripides' *Cyclops* other than
a symposiastic drinking scene, in which Polyphemus complains to
Odysseus, 'You ruined the wine by pouring in water' (*TrGF* 4).[55] But
in the remaining fragments of Cratinus' *Odysseis*, Polyphemus reveals
an interest in preparing food much like Euripides' Cyclops:[56]

ἀνθ' ὧν πάντας ἑλὼν ὑμᾶς ἐρίηρας ἑταίρους,
φρύξας, Χἀψήσας, κἀπ' ἀνθρακιᾶς κὠπτήσας

εἰς ἅλμην τε καὶ ὀξάλμην κᾆτ' ἐς σκοροδάλμην
χλιαρὸν ἐμβάπτων, ὃς ἂν ὀπτότατός μοι ἁπάντων
ὑμῶν φαίνηται, κατατρώξομαι, ὦ στρατιῶται.

Cratinus K-A 150, trans. Storey 2011

In return for which I shall seize all you 'loyal comrades', roast you, boil you, barbecue and bake you, dip you into brine and vinegar and warm garlic sauce, and whichever of you soldiers appears to be the best cooked, that's the one I shall munch down.

Cratinus' version of Polyphemus' cannibalistic dinner focuses on methods of cooking that anticipate Euripides' *Cyclops*, with similar mention of roasting, boiling, and baking on coals:

ὡς ἕτοιμά σοι
ἑφθὰ καὶ ὀπτὰ καὶ ἀνθρακιᾶς ἄπο <θερμὰ>
χναύειν βρύκειν
κρεοκοπεῖν μέλη ξένων

Euripides *Cyclops* 358–9

> The limbs of the guests
> are boiled and broiled and warm
> from the coals, ready for you
> to gnaw, devour, and chop.

Cratinus' Polyphemus, though, is even more exhaustive in the details of his feast, mentioning brines, vinegars, and sauces to flavour the men. He also mentions 'large suckling pigs' (K-A 154) and 'a warm slice of sea perch' (K-A 155), comical references to a feast that eclipses the rather straightforward human dinner found in Homer's *Odyssey* and in Euripides' *Cyclops*.

The fragments of Callias' *Cyclopes*, which was performed in 434, offers a similarly food-focused production that seems both to look backward to the plays of Cratinus, Aristias, and Epicharmus and forward to Euripides' *Cyclops*. Like Cratinus, Callias is more exploratory in the language of the feast, particularly with the emphasis on seafood:

κίθαρος ὀπτὸς καὶ βατὶς θύννου τε κεφάλαιον τοδί,
ἐγχέλεια, κάραβοι, λινεύς, ἀχαρνὼς οὑτοσί.

Callias I K-A 6, trans. Storey (2011)

Roasted flatfish and skate and here's a head of tuna,
eel, crayfish, mullet, and here's a sea bass

The way in which Callias and Cratinus expand Homer's version of Polyphemus' feast corresponds to comedy's typical, exaggerated mode of reinterpreting myth. This is especially true in the references to fish, since seafoods were considered unheroic and un-epic, but very comical.[57] Callias (K-A 12) is similarly over the top in representing in his play the kottabos, a sympotic game (in which participants fling the dregs of wine at a target) that is often found in comedy, but not in Homer's works.[58] Euripides plays with the myth in a self-conscious, meta-mythological manner, but not in the outrageous style of comedy.

Ultimately, it is impossible to tie Euripides' production directly to any of the prior theatrical performances, whether comic or satyric, Athenian or Sicilian; but given Euripides' particular interest in the literary precedents for the myth and (as we will see) literary models outside the plot of the *Cyclops*, it seems quite likely that he was inspired in one way or another by Epicharmus, Aristias, Cratinus, and Callias in his own adaptation of the myth. Each of the productions about Odysseus' encounter with Polyphemus treats food and wine, and it is even more significant *how* they deal with these items.[59] In all instances, there is a focus on wine and food preparation that does not occur in the original source material. It was no doubt amusing to see the Cyclops consistently portrayed not as a beastly cannibal, but as a contemporary gourmand. Polyphemus always takes part in the basic elements of the myth, but he is updated to reflect fifth-century *opsophagoi*, lovers of various foods and fine dining. Euripides seems to draw upon his predecessor's plays and even further rewrites the myth as he pushes the comic-satyric symposium into fresh territory with an offstage erotic scene between Silenus and the monster (vv. 582–3).[60]

Other drama: Sophocles' *Philoctetes*, Aristophanes' *Thesmophoriazusae*, and Euripides' *Helen, Andromeda,* and *Iphigenia among the Taurians*

Euripides places his *Cyclops* in the tradition of comic-satyric exploration of myth, with creative and subtle literary references to Homer, the Homeric Hymns, and earlier comic and satyric productions of the Polyphemus-Odysseus story. There also appears to be a parodic/comedic relationship with certain Athenian tragedies and comedies outside of the relevant myth, including Sophocles' *Philoctetes*, Aristophanes' *Thesmophoriazusae*, and Euripides' own *Helen, Andromeda,* and *Iphigenia among the Taurians*. Unfortunately, the exact date of Euripides' *Cyclops* is unknown, but it is most likely between 412 and 408, the same years in which these various plays were staged. Because of the chronological proximity of performances, it is difficult to distinguish the direction of some of these relationships. Therefore, in the first part of this section, I will explore the *Cyclops'* relationship to these plays under the assumption that it was performed in 408, the most widely accepted date of performance for Euripides' satyr play. In the second part, I will turn to an attractive argument that dates the *Cyclops* to 412 and alters our understanding of the various intertextual relationships.

Sophocles' *Philoctetes* was performed in 409 and presents the attempt of Odysseus and Achilles' son Neoptolemus to bring the disabled and spurned hero Philoctetes to Troy.[61] As many scholars have noted, there appears to be an intertext between Euripides' *Cyclops* and Sophocles' tragedy in the use of a particular phrase, δι' ἀμφιτρῆτος (through the double-doored cave). Sophocles and Euripides are the only two ancient authors to use the word ἀμφιτρής, ῆτος, ὁ, ἡ (rock *pierced through*, cave *with double entrance*), and both use the same phrase in the same metrical *sedes* within a few years of each other:

δι᾿ ἀμφιτρῆτος τῆσδε προσβαίνων ποδί.

Euripides' *Cyclops* 707.

going on foot through the double-doored cave.

δι᾿ ἀμφιτρῆτος αὐλίου πέμπει πνοή·

Sophocles' *Philoctetes* 19.

the wind blows through the double-doored cave.

If Euripides' play was performed in 408, the use of this phrase is very likely a reference to Sophocles' *Philoctetes*. Euripides' choice to place it in Polyphemus' final speech is interesting and possibly parodic/critical,[62] but no scholars have been able to offer a convincing explanation for this particular intertext.[63] Nevertheless, the plays present a number of seemingly meaningful literary connections. In addition to using the same rare phrase, they correspond in their use of Odysseus as a main character, in their setting by a cave on a rocky island, and in their use of an ogre-ish/disfigured character who is both savage and divine (Polyphemus through his parentage and Philoctetes through his wound).[64] And as Marshall notes, Odysseus in both plays aims to accomplish the challenging task of 're-integration of the individual into society'.[65]

Euripides' satyr play also presents a fascinating intertext with Euripides' own tragic *Andromeda* (412) and Aristophanes' comic *Thesmophoriazusae* (411). Although the *Andromeda* is lost, a few fragments remain, and most of the plot can be reconstructed fairly confidently, but it is the start of the play that is most relevant for our discussion. In the play's opening scene, Andromeda is chained to a rock near a cave where she will serve as a sacrifice to a sea monster. When Perseus first walks onstage, he believes that she is a statue:

ἔα, τίν' ὄχθον τόνδ' ὁρῶ περίρρυτον
ἀφρῷ θαλάσσης; παρθένου δ' εἰκὼ τίνα,
ἐξ αὐτομόρφων λαΐνων τυκισμάτων
σοφῆς ἄγαλμα χειρός;

> Euripides, *Andromeda* fr. 125, trans. adapted from Collard and
> Cropp 2008

Oho, what crag is this I see, lapped
by sea-foam, and what maiden's likeness,
a statue carved by an expert hand to her
very form in stone?

Euripides' *Andromeda* was (in)famous in antiquity,[66] and Aristophanes referred to it at least twice, including in the *Thesmophoriazusae*, which was performed the following year, in 411.

Ἔα, τιν' ὄχθον τόνδ' ὁρῶ καὶ παρθένον
θεαῖς ὁμοίαν ναῦν ὅπως ὡρμισμένην;

> Aristophanes, *Thesmophoriazusae* 1105–6,
> trans. Henderson 2000

Oho, what crag is this I see? What maiden,
fair as a goddess, moored like a boat thereto?

Although the intertext does not appear particularly interesting at first glance, Aristophanes' comedy actually includes Euripides as a character and the tragedian speaks these very verses.[67] In addition, the whole scene is a parody of Euripides' tragedy. Euripides' kinsman has been caught infiltrating a women's festival, and Euripides, as Perseus, shows up and tries to rescue him as he acts the part of Andromeda. Here we have, then, a rather remarkable parody: Aristophanes' version of Euripides is dressed as Perseus and quotes Euripides' own version of Perseus.

If the *Cyclops* was performed in 408, Euripides is creating an intertext not with his own *Andromeda*, but with Aristophanes' parody of *Andromeda*. Polyphemus walks onstage and shouts:

ἔα· τίν' ὄχλον τόνδ' ὁρῶ πρὸς αὐλίοις;

Euripides, *Cyclops* 222

Oho! What crowd is this I see near my cave?

The complexity and inventiveness of these intertexts is remarkable, as Euripides turns traditional modes of parody on their head: Euripides (a tragedian) parodies Aristophanes' comic parody of Euripides' tragedy in his satyr play.[68] The *Cyclops* also inverts the effect of the scene. In *Andromeda* and *Thesmophoriazusae*, the Greek 'hero' (both Perseus and Euripides as Perseus) views a foreign land with surprise, but in Euripides' *Cyclops*, the foreign monster Polyphemus views his own familiar home with surprise: 'It is no longer the figure within the barbarian landscape that is held up as strange, but the Greeks themselves.'[69]

Although most scholars see Aristophanes parodying Euripides' *Andromeda* (412) in his *Thesmophoriazusae* (411), and then Euripides answering that parody in his *Cyclops* (408),[70] Wright makes a compelling case for the *Cyclops* to be dated to the same tetralogy as the *Andromeda* in 412. In this way, Euripides would be parodying his own tragedy on the same day just hours after the audience heard Perseus utter his lines. It would be playful and humorous and much more immediate and memorable than a three- to four-year-old allusion. In addition, the *Cyclops*' plot fits well with Wright's proposal that Euripides' trilogy of 412 consisted of three escape-themed tragedies: *Helen*, *Andromeda*, and *Iphigenia among the Taurians*.[71] The *Cyclops* presents certain intertexts and similarities in plots and themes with this trilogy, offering the sort of engagement that would shed a 'crucial revelatory or ironic light on the preceding tragic action'.[72]

Without a single complete tetralogy, it is impossible to know the depth of the relationship between tragedies and their subsequent satyr plays, but it is clear that most tragic trilogies probably did not have the sort of connected plot that is found in Aeschylus' *Oresteia*.[73] That said, it would be surprising if there were not thematic connections between and amongst the plays of a given tetralogy, even if the plots were not connected.[74] The opportunity to explore complex ideas over the course of four plays would be exciting and effective, as Aeschylus' *Oresteia* demonstrates with its exploration of monarchy, tyranny, and democracy over the course of the trilogy. This thematic relationship would presumably continue even into the satyr play. In fact, as the final play in a tetralogy, a satyric performance would perhaps have been considered the culminating opportunity to comment on themes explored in a tetralogy, whether it reinforced or parodied those themes.[75] If the *Cyclops* was staged in 412, it seems that Euripides established this sort of complex relationship between his satyr play and the preceding trilogy of tragedies.

Matthew Wright (2005) has suggested that Euripides' *Helen, Andromeda,* and *Iphigenia among the Taurians* were performed together at the City Dionysia of 412.[76] He finds a significant overlap in their interest in mythological self-consciousness, cultural identity, sophistic philosophy, and geographical location. In his follow-up study, Wright demonstrates that Euripides is equally interested in these particular themes in his *Cyclops*, and suggests that it too was performed this year, offering a chronology that corresponds to the range of dates championed by most scholars (412–408).[77] In terms of 'metamythological' exploration, Euripides' *Helen, Andromeda,* and *Iphigenia among the Taurians* depict mythological figures self-consciously reflecting upon their own mythical backgrounds. As we saw at the start of the chapter, the characters and the chorus of the *Cyclops* present a similarly extensive knowledge of Odysseus' original Homeric myth. Euripides is also obsessed with the location of the story in each of his tragedies, and all are situated on distant, unwelcoming shores a long way from Greece. This is similar to Euripides' choice to place Polyphemus and the Cyclopes on the rocky coast near Mt. Aetna in Sicily, a point he mentions repeatedly throughout the play.[78] In all four of these plays, Euripides also delves into the relationship between the civilized and uncivilized at the marginal, liminal space of the seashore, exploring the remoteness of the Greeks in these barbarian lands.

In addition to the similar themes found in all four plays, Euripides also presents similar plots, with each production focusing on escape. In each of the tragic plays, Euripides draws out the similarity of situation, even though the plots present different characters and myths. The tragedies explore the futility of escape, suggesting a certain endless circularity of imprisonment and flight which is followed again by imprisonment. This plays out in a particularly interesting way in the *Cyclops*, since the satyrs are endlessly captured and enslaved in the genre of satyr drama, as they forever switch between being slaves to an ogre and slaves to Dionysus. The satyrs live out the perpetual escape-enslavement cycle, thereby providing a powerful conclusion to the preceding tragedies, especially in the satyrs' final couplet (708–9), which has important religious overtones: the only true escape from enslavement is the willing service to the god Dionysus.

Ultimately, the literary relationship between these plays and their connection as a complete tetralogy is unprovable, but the *Cyclops* does demonstrate certain associations with *Helen*, *Andromeda*, and *Iphigenia among the Taurians*. And as we have seen throughout this chapter, Euripides is fond of exploring literary relationships in his *Cyclops*, which suggests that he would also have had a similar interest in creating literary connections to his preceding trilogy of tragedies. If the *Cyclops* was, in fact, the final play in 412 after the *Helen*, *Andromeda*, and *Iphigenia among the Taurians*, it presumably functioned as a response of sorts to the previous plays.[79] By exploring the themes of his own preceding trilogy of tragedies in the *Cyclops*, Euripides would transform his satyr play into a culminating theatrical performance that served as part religious production, part humorous burlesque, and part social and literary commentary.

If the *Cyclops* was performed in 412, it would also mean that Euripides was not creating an intertext with Sophocles' *Philoctetes*, but that Sophocles (*Philoctetes*, v. 19) was parodying Euripides' use of δι' ἀμφιτρῆτος (*Cyclops* 707).[80] This parody could be attributed to the fact that Euripides' use of a cave with a 'double-entrance' is a significant plot hole for the *Cyclops*. As Polyphemus exits the stage for the last time, he says that he plans to go through the cave to throw boulders at Odysseus' ship. The idea that Polyphemus could run through the cave and exit the other side suggests that Odysseus and his men were never trapped at all. Given the limitations of the theatre at this time, the use of an open cave entrance onstage makes a great deal of sense, but the use of a second cave entrance on the back side undermines the entire plot of the play. If Sophocles was referring to Euripides' *Cyclops* in his *Philoctetes*, then he was likely drawing attention to a major flaw in Euripides' version of the story.

This particular chronology would also transform our understanding of parody in the Euripides-Aristophanes literary dynamic.[81] It would mean that Aristophanes was parodying Euripides' own parody of himself, since Euripides uses ἔα, τίν' ὄχθον τόνδ' ὁρῶ (Oho! What crag is this I see?) in *Andromeda* and ἔα· τίν' ὄχλον τόνδ' ὁρῶ (Oho, what crowd is this I see?) in the *Cyclops*, two very similar phrases in the same tetralogy. Euripides draws attention to his own previous scene, linking Andromeda not with Odysseus and the Greeks, but with the sheep that are bound up in front of Polyphemus' cave. And this reference, it turns out, provides one more playful revision of Homer's original. Polyphemus says:

ἔα· τίν' ὄχλον τόνδ' ὁρῶ πρὸς αὐλίοις;
λῃσταί τινες κατέσχον ἢ κλῶπες χθόνα;
ὁρῶ γέ τοι τούσδ' ἄρνας ἐξ ἄντρων ἐμῶν
στρεπταῖς λύγοισι σῶμα συμπεπλεγμένους

Euripides, *Cyclops* 222–7

Oho! What crowd is this I see near my cave?
Have some pirates or thieves occupied this land?
I see lambs from my cave out here,
with their bodies bound together with woven withes

Polyphemus' language in this passage, with the binding and tying of the sheep, is reminiscent of the *Andromeda*, but it also functions as a reference to Homer's *Odyssey* (429–31), where Odysseus and his men escape from the Cyclops' cave under sheep that are tied together in threes. Euripides is unable to act out the original version of the myth because of the challenges of staging such an elaborate scene (also, there is no reason to be so elaborate, since the cave is not blocked by a boulder), but he still retains the scene in a humorously unpredictable manner. He preserves Homer's myth, playing with chronology and plot. Silenus (like the poet and the audience) knows that when Homer's sheep leave Polyphemus' cave they are supposed to be bound together in threes, so he ties them up and presents the traditional story at the wrong time in the narrative. Euripides rewrites Homer's *Odyssey* again in a comedic, playful, glib, and self-consciously literary manner.

Conclusion

In Chapter 3, we saw Euripides bring the myth of Odysseus and Polyphemus into the contemporary world, by incorporating and addressing contemporary Athenian issues, such as philosophy, politics, and the theatre. But given the *Cyclops*' generically self-conscious and self-referential mode, it was also prone to literary allusions, intertexts, and analyses. Euripides highlights satyr drama's historical relationship with comedy by including 'comedic' jokes, but also by placing the *Cyclops* in constant dialogue with comedy and satyr drama as *kômos*-song. The *Cyclops* even acknowledges a certain awareness of its genre and its genre's relationship to comedy through literary criticism. Euripides establishes the *Cyclops* as the greatest satyr play in the history of satyr plays, and works to surpass the Homeric prototype by alluding to, altering, and 'improving' the *Odyssey*. He adapts book nine of Homer's *Odyssey* fairly faithfully, but he makes certain changes based on the limitations of the stage, while other changes seem more calculated (some of these were seen in the previous chapter with Euripides' incorporation of religious and historical themes). In addition to rewriting Homer, Euripides incorporates the myth of the *Homeric Hymn to Dionysus* into that of the *Odyssey*, as he works within the comic-satyric tradition of earlier Odysseus-Polyphemus plays. The *Cyclops* is not nearly as over the top as Cratinus' and Callias' comedies, but like its comic and satyric predecessors, it does focus on Polyphemus' feast and pseudo-symposium. Euripides even creates intertexts outside the myth(s) of the *Cyclops'* plot and outside the tradition of comedies and satyr plays. He establishes a generic relationship between satyr drama and comedy that informs all other literary relationships, even, it seems, his own tragedies in the tetralogy of 412.

In many ways, Euripides' *Cyclops* is a modest play, about half the length of most Greek tragedies, a quaint mythological drama preserved not for its reputation in antiquity, but by a happy accident in the textual tradition. Nevertheless, as the only complete satyr play, it is one of the most important ancient Athenian theatrical productions to have been passed down to modern audiences. Satyr plays were performed three times each year at Athens' greatest religious and civic festival, after a tragedian's three tragedies, and alongside comedy and dithyramb. As such, satyr plays engaged with Dionysiac religion and contemporary social issues, provided a place for reflection on literature, myth, and performance, and served as the final reminder of a poet's skills before judging took place. Euripides' *Cyclops* thrives under the burden of being its genre's only extant representative, providing an invaluable glimpse at the complexities of satyr drama in its various contexts. In his satyr play, Euripides explores the genre's religious and historical relationship with Dionysiac performance and ritual. He toys with satyr drama's generic relationship to comedy (and dithyramb and tragedy). He updates one of the most famous Homeric stories for the Athenian stage, rewriting an archaic myth to fit contemporary society. And he uses the genre's repetitive and self-consciously performative nature to develop an epic tale into a relevant vehicle for playful literary criticism and analysis. Despite the numerous uncertainties that remain, Euripides' *Cyclops* presents an invaluable picture of satyr drama and the theatrical experience as a whole in fifth-century Athens.

Notes

Chapter 1

1   The festival was scheduled from the ninth to the thirteenth of the lunar month Elaphebolion. On festival chronology, see Csapo and Slater (1995, 105–8).

2   The annexation of Eleutherae probably occurred around the time of Cleisthenes' democratic reforms in the last quarter of the sixth century, when Athens transitioned to a democracy. On the foundation of the City Dionysia, see Pickard-Cambridge (1968), Csapo and Slater (1995, 103–21), and Wilson (2007).

3   Scholion to Aristophanes, *Acharnians* 243. The disease sent by Dionysus was most likely permanent ithyphallicism, but may have been impotence. Cf. Csapo and Slater (1995, 110–11).

4   See Csapo and Slater (1995, 104) for details of the phallophoria.

5   Wilson (2000) provides an excellent study of nearly every element of choral productions in Athens.

6   On Dithyramb, see Pickard-Cambridge (1962), Zimmermann (1992), Ieranò (1997), Pritchard (2004), and Kowalzig and Wilson (2013).

7   The number of comic poets probably fluctuated due to the availability of funds. During financially secure times, there were five comic poets, but during leaner times, only three. Also, some scholars suspect that the comedies were distributed over multiple days. For a useful, recent collection of essays overviewing Greek comedy, see Revermann (2014).

8   Most of our extant tragic plays were performed at this festival. For more on Greek tragedy, see Pickard-Cambridge (1962), Easterling (1997a), and Rehm (2017).

9   The foremost works on satyr drama include Sutton (1980), Seaford (1984), Conrad (1997), Pechstein (1998), KPS (1999), Voelke (2001), Cipolla (2003), Napolitano (2003), Harrison (2005b), O'Sullivan and Collard (2013), Lämmle (2013), Shaw (2014), and Griffith (2015).

10   Lissarrague (1990b, 236).

11   Euripides' *Alcestis* is the only known play to be performed in the fourth
       position of a tetralogy without a chorus of satyrs. See Slater (2013) and
       Chapter 4 for more on the anomalous nature of *Alcestis*.

12   For an excellent, recent overview of the ambiguities and complexities
       of satyrs, see O'Sullivan and Collard (2013, 8–22). Cf. Voelke (2001,
       53–90), who studies the satyr as a 'figure de l'intermédiare'.

13   Traditionally, satyrs were man-horse creatures, but through time –
       perhaps through associations with the god Pan – they began to be
       thought of and depicted as goat-men. Even during the classical period,
       texts sometimes make reference to the goat-like qualities, as does
       Cyllene in Sophocles' *Ichneutae* (v. 367). Cf. Hedreen (1992, 163).

14   It is often very difficult to distinguish depictions of mythological satyrs
       from depictions of performative satyrs, particularly because artists
       regularly merged costume elements with the performer's body. On
       the challenges of classifying representations of satyrs, see Lissarrague
       (1990, 228–36), Hedreen (1992, esp. 125–78, and 2007), Steinhart
       (2004, 101–27), Green (2007, 101 and 104–5), and Csapo (2010, 5).
       Athenian theatrical performances in particular seem to have used a
       smaller stage phallus. Compare, for example, the satyrs on the archaic
       François Vase (Figure 1.1) with those on the classical-age Pronomos
       Vase (Figure 2.1). On the satyr's form, see Seaford (1984, 5–10), KPS
       (1999, 19), as well as Hedreen (1992 and 2007), who prefers the term
       'silen' to 'satyr'. Keuls (1993, 68) observes that the satyrs' large phallus is
       a sign of their bestiality, not hyper-sexuality. On the sexuality of satyrs,
       see (Lissarrague 1990a and 1993), Keuls (1993, 65–97; 357–78), Stewart
       (1997, 187–92), Hall (1998), and Voelke (2001, 211–59).

15   Fr. 10a.18 MW. Hesiod's floruit is traditionally dated to the late eighth
       or early seventh centuries.

16   In the fourth century, Theopompus (115 *FGrH* 775c.3-4), for example,
       remarks that Silenus, the father of the satyrs, is immortal and superior
       to humankind.

17   Aeschylus' *Dionysou Trophoi* (*TrGF* 3, F246a-d) and Sophocles'
       Dionysiskos (*TrGF* 4 F171-3).

18 Aristotle, *Eudemus* F44 Rose. Cf. Herodotus, *Histories* 8.138.

19 Seaford (1984, 6) says that what we call "'satyrs" might be more accurately called "satyr-silens". On silens, see above all the work of Hedreen (1992, 2007).

20 Hedreen (2004) offers a valuable study on the Return of Hephaestus and satyrs/silens.

21 Hedreen (1992, 137–8, 2007, 162–3).

22 Consider also Socrates' external and internal similarities to satyr-silens in Plato's *Symposium* (215a–221d) and Xenophon's *Symposium* (6.1).

23 For a detailed treatment of the formal and conceptual connections between tragedy and satyr play, see esp. Griffith (2002, 2005, 166–72, 2010), Seaford (1984, 44–8), and KPS (1999, 12–34). Ion of Chios (*c.* 490–420, *ap.* Plutarch, *Per.* 5.3) demonstrates the seeming necessity of tragic and satyric associations in his explanation of *arete* (excellence): 'Like a tragic production, excellence should have its share of the satyric.'

24 Sophocles' *Poimenes* (*Shepherds*) is one of the most famous examples. For full discussion, with bibliography, see Rosen (2003). Cf. Griffith (2006, 52).

25 On the relationship between comedy and satyr drama, see Shaw (2014).

26 During the fifth century, Ecphantides, Cratinus (twice), Callias, and Phrynichus staged comedies with a chorus of satyrs; during the fourth century, Timocles (twice) and, perhaps, Ophelio also offered 'satyr comedies'. On comedy's use of satyrs, see Storey (2005) and Shaw (2014, 90–4).

27 Foley (2014) offers a helpful discussion of the issues of 'Performing Gender' in Greek comedy.

28 Shaw (2014, 3).

29 Innes in Halliwell et al. (1995, 312–21) provides details on the date and authorship of Demetrius' treatise. Few descriptions of satyr drama are extant. Aristotle's student Chamaeleon wrote a work on satyr drama, *Peri Satyrôn*, but it has not survived.

30 See, for example, section headings in Seaford (1984, 1–5) and O'Sullivan and Collard (2013, 1–8), as well as the title for a collection of essays on satyr drama edited by Harrison (2005b).

31 Griffith (2008, 76–7) presents the most thorough discussion of Demetius' remarks. Cf. Shaw (2014, 13–14).

32 On the early stages of satyr drama, with relevant bibliography, see Shaw (2014, 26–55).

33 Seaford (1984, 13) and Hedreen (1992, 125–8).

34 Differentiating mythological scenes from performative scenes on ancient vases is a fraught issue with a significant bibliography. Hedreen (1992, esp. 125–78 and 2007) provides the most sensible guidelines. For a detailed discussion of this challenging problem, along with bibliography, see Shaw (2014, 27 n. 4).

35 KPS (1999, 41–73) provides a full discussion of archaeological evidence for satyr drama, including this vase.

36 Artists often blended the mask and costume into the performer's body in this way. Even on the Pronomos Vase (Figure 2.1), there is no particular sign that the masked choreut is wearing a mask.

37 For a useful introduction and extensive bibliography on Pratinas, see O'Sullivan and Collard (2013). Cf. Shaw (2014, 43–55).

38 See *TrGF* 1².

39 The 'hyporcheme' is a difficult term to define because it broadly refers to a song and dance performed at the same time. On these challenges, see Mathieson (1999, 88–94). Athenaeus explains the quarrel about the *aulos'* role in his *Deipnosophistae*: 'Pipe-players did not play music to accompany the choruses, as was traditional, but the choruses instead sang to accompany the pipes', trans. Olson (2011, 14.617b). Cf. Shaw (2014, 51–4).

40 On Dionysus' role in satyr drama, see especially Seaford (1976, 1981), Easterling (1997b), Griffith (2002), Bierl (2006), Lämmle (2007).

41 For Aeschylus' *Theoroi* or *Isthmiastae* (*TrGF* 3 F78a–82), see Sommerstein (2008, 82–99) and for Sophocles' *Dionysiskos* (*TrGF* 4² F171–3), see Lloyd-Jones (2013, 66–7).

42 Chapter 3 offers a comprehensive discussion of Dionysus' importance in the *Cyclops*, where he figures prominently, despite the fact that he is not a character.

43 Although fragmentary, Sophocles' *Ichneutae*, or *Trackers* (*TrGF* 4²
   F314–318), provides our best evidence for satyr drama after Euripides'
   Cyclops. Anyone interested in the genre should consult the play, which
   is most easily accessed in Lloyd-Jones' (2003) Loeb edition of *Sophocles
   Fragments*. For a helpful discussion and essential bibliography, see
   O'Sullivan and Collard (2013, 336–43).

44 On typical plots and themes, see Sutton (1980, 145–59), Seaford (1984,
   33–9), KPS (1999, 28–32), Voelke (2001, 377–81), and O'Sullivan and
   Collard (2013, 28–39).

45 On Aeschylus' *Proteus*, see Sommerstein (2008, 220–3) and for a fuller,
   hypothetical discussion, Griffith (2002).

46 On late classical and post-classical satyr drama, see Shaw (2014,
   123–48).

47 *IG* II² 2320; Millis and Olson (2012, 61–9).

48 *Poetics*, 1447b, 21. The *Centaur* cannot be labelled a satyr play with
   certainty. Cf. Collard (1970), Morelli (2001), Shaw (2014, 130–3).

49 Kaimio (2001, 59) and Shaw (2014, 133–4).

50 On satyr drama's shift towards satire, see van Rooy (1965), Xanthakis-
   Karamanos (1997), Cozzoli (2003), and Shaw (2014, 136–9).

51 For discussion of this play and its historical context, see Sutton (1980,
   75–81), Cipolla (2003, 347–60), Pretagostini (2003), O'Sullivan and
   Collard (2013, 448–55), and Shaw (2014, 123–9).

52 Shaw (2014, 144–5) catalogues the various inscriptions that note late
   satyric performances.

53 The study of satyrs in Rome has not garnered a great deal of attention.
   Cf. Wiseman (1988) and Shaw (145–8).

54 For recent discussions of satyr drama's functions (including useful
   surveys and original theories), see Seaford (1984, 26–33), Lissarrague
   (1990a), Hall (1998, 2006, 142–69), KPS (1999, 34–39), Voelke (2001),
   Gibert (2002), and Griffith (2002, 2005), Lämmle (2013, 93–98). In
   the introduction to his *Trackers of Oxyrhynchus*, a re-imagining of
   Sophocles' satyr play *Ichneutae* (*Trackers*), Tony Harrison (1990, xi)
   offers a poetic and powerful reminder of the importance of satyr drama

to the original performance: 'With the loss of these [satyr] plays we are lacking important clues to the wholeness of the Greek imagination, and its ability to absorb and yet not be defeated by the tragic.' Cf. Easterling (1997b).

55 Hall (1998, 2006, 142–69). Extant tragedies often consider the relationship between women and the polis in striking and powerful ways. As the final play in a tetralogy, satyr drama would function as a sort of hyper-masculine corrective to the preceding three tragedies.

56 Cf. Seaford (1976, 1981), Easterling (1997b), Griffith (2002), Bierl (2006), and Lämmle (2007).

57 On Aristotle and the origins of drama, see Pickard-Cambridge (1962, 96–7), Lord (1974), Herington (1985), Nagy (1990, 385–8), Leonhardt (1991), and Seaford (2007, 379), who states that 'any serious account … must start from what Aristotle reports in his *Poetics* about the genesis of drama'. On Aristotle and satyr drama in particular, see Cozzoli (2003, 268–9), Depew (2007), and Griffith (2008).

58 Seaford (1984, 10–12, 2007, 381).

59 See Depew (2007) for an excellent study of 'Aristotle's Genealogy of Poetic Kinds'.

60 For example, we know that both Aeschylus (*Persians*, 474) and Phrynichus (*Capture of Miletus*, *c*. 494) composed tragedies on recent historical events rather than mythological tales, and others composed tragedies with happy endings. Wright (2016, 1–28) provides a helpful examination of 'The Earliest Tragedies'.

61 On the relationship between Dionysiac ritual and drama, see especially Pickard-Cambridge (1962), Burkert (1966), Winkler and Zeitlin (1990), Seaford (1994), Easterling (1997b), Sourvinou-Inwood (2003), and Csapo and Miller (2007, 1–32).

62 In his work *On Thespis*, Chamaeleon (F 38 Wehrli) also refers to pre-theatrical performances named *satyrika* that evolved into non-Dionysiac tragedy, but because he was a student of Aristotle, it is difficult to disentangle Peripatetic knowledge from Peripatetic theories. Second century CE Zenobius (5.40 = Ieranò 1997 no. 65) offers a similar version of the 'Nothing to do with Dionysus' anecdote: "After

that time, when, from the beginning, choruses were accustomed to sing the dithyramb to Dionysus, poets later departed from this habit, and put their hand to writing 'Ajaxes' and 'Centaurs'. Because of this the spectators joking around said, 'Nothing to do with Dionysus'. For this reason it seemed good to them later to introduce satyr plays as a prelude, so that they might not seem to be forgetful of the god".

63 Aeschylus' *Theoroi* or *Isthmiastae* (*TrGF* 3 F78a-82), *Diktyulkoi* (*TrGF* 3 F161-74), and *Dionysou Trophoi* (*TrGF* 3, F246a-d) respectively.

64 Burkert (1985, 161–6).

65 See Chapter 4 for discussion of the relationship between Euripides' *Cyclops* and Homer's *Odyssey*.

66 Homer, *Odyssey* 9.174–6. Trans. Murray/Dimock (1995).

67 For more on the 'Nobody' trick, see Chapter 4.

68 Homer, *Odyssey* 9.408. Trans. Murray/Dimock (1995).

69 Pucci (1998, 114–30) presents an interesting theoretical study of Odysseus' inability to remain 'Nobody'.

70 On the date of the *Cyclops*, see the recent overview with relevant bibliography in O'Sullivan and Collard (2013, 39–41).

71 Seaford (1982) and Wright (2006). For a more detailed discussion of the *Cyclops*' date and its relevance to the play's literary relationships, see Chapter 4.

72 Seaford (1984) provides a complete account of the *Cyclops*' textual transmission.

73 Zuntz (1965).

74 See O'Sullivan and Collard's (2013) *apparatus criticus* at 69, 181, 510, 514, 604.

75 Oxyrhynchus Papyri Vol. LXVII (2001) 16–18, No. 4545 includes the ends of verses 455–71 and 484–96, as well as the openings of 479–81.

76 In the example just quoted, it seems likely that one person read the text aloud, while another wrote, since Διὸς and βοὸς sound more similar than they look. Reynolds and Wilson (2014) offer an excellent overview of transmission of texts from antiquity.

77 Any performances that did not comply were considered illegal. Plutarch *Vitae Decem Oratorum* 851e.

78 Most likely under Ptolemy III Euergetes, 247–221. Cf. Fraser (1972, vol. I, 325).

Chapter 2

1 Cf. Taplin (1985, 7–14) on the absence of stage directions and on 'Stage Management and Action' more generally.

2 Vitruvius, *De Architectura* (5.6.9).

3 On ancient Athenian staging techniques, see various contributions in Harrison and Liapis (2013).

4 For evidence, see Csapo and Slater (1995, 64–5 I 131, pl. 4B).

5 Scholars have proposed a wide range of sizes for the audience at the fifth-century City Dionysia, from 4,000–7,000 to 10,000–15,000. See Csapo (2007, 97–100).

6 On the Pronomos Vase, see the excellent collection of essays in Taplin and Wyles (2010).

7 Lissarrague (1990a, b, and 1993) examines these characteristics of satyrs.

8 See below for a more detailed discussion of Silenus' use of the phallus in the play.

9 On props in Greek drama, see Revermann (2013, 77–88).

10 Csapo and Slater (1995, 105).

11 Euripides takes this plot from the *Homeric Hymn to Dionysus*. See Chapter 4 for more on the combination of Homer's *Odyssey* and the *Homeric Hymn*.

12 Seaford (1977, 84, 1984, 92); Harrison (2005a).

13 See Chapters 3 and 4 on the religious and literary significance of *kômos* in the *Cyclops*.

14 On the *sikinnis*, see Festa (1918, esp. 51–70), Lawler (1964), and Seidensticker (2010).

15 See, for example, the one satyr choreut wearing his mask on the Pronomos Vase (Figure 2.1).

16 Lissarrague (1990b, 55–7).

17 Verse 40. Cf. Lissarrague (1993, 212), who helpfully notes that 'satyrs are represented in perpetual movement, as though they were incapable of controlling their bodies'.

18 On the theme of friendship (*philia*), see Ambrose (2005). On the satyrs as perpetual slaves, see Griffith (2002).

19 Cf. Sophocles *Ichneutae* (v. 367), where Cyllene compares the satyrs to goats. After the classical period, satyrs were thought of as more goat-like, perhaps due to associations with the goat-god Pan.

20 Burkert (1966) suggests that tragedy evolved from songs performed at the sacrifice of a goat, or where a goat was the prize for the victor.

21 Taplin (1977, 129) says, 'there were silent extras all over the place in Greek tragedy'.

22 Polyphemus would consume any humans who happened to land on his island, and he goes out of his way in verses 220–1 to explain why he has not eaten the satyrs, saying, 'Not a chance I would do that! You'd destroy me with your dancing, jumping around inside my stomach.' In addition to giving a sense of the satyrs' nonstop leaping and dancing during the play, these verses also seal a very serious potential hole in the plot: Why hasn't the cannibalistic Cyclops eaten the satyrs?

23 According to *Odyssey* 9.266–71, 'hospitality' is a sacred concept to Zeus. For more on *xenia*, see Chapter 3.

24 Goldhill (1997, 127–8).

25 Wright (2006). See Chapter 4 for a full discussion of Silenus' meta-mythological awareness.

26 On Odysseus' alternate genealogy, see Gantz (1993, 175–6), who lists and discusses the various sources for this tradition.

27 Aristotle (*Nicomachean Ethics* 1128a): 'The lawgivers forbid any *loidorein* (raillery, abuse), and it ought to be the same with *skeptein* (mocking, jesting, jeering).'

28 Stephen Halliwell (1991) examines this distinction between playful and abusive (or 'consequential') modes of humour. Many Greek philosophers express their concerns about this type of joke. Cf. Plato *Laws* (11.935d–6a).

29 West (1982) provides a helpful guide to Greek meter.
30 For other ways in which Silenus is a poet-figure, see Torrance (2013, 256–7).
31 On satyrs and wine, see Lissarrague (1990, passim).
32 Anacreon fr. 31 Page. For Sappho's legend, see Strabo 10.2.9.
33 Verses 170–1. For further discussion of these jokes with relevant bibliography, see Chapter 4. On the hyper-masculine nature of satyr drama more generally, see Hall's (1998) study of 'Ithyphallic Males Behaving Badly.'
34 See Chapter 4 for further discussion of humorous, comedic diction in the *Cyclops*.
35 Cf. Kerényi (1996).
36 Verses 201–2. See Chapter 4 for further discussion of these verses.
37 Trendall (1989, 19–20) notes 'the artist's emphasis on the theatrical aspect'. Cf. Green and Handley (1995, 112). Carpenter (2005, 226–7), however, argues that artists worked more independently of performances.
38 In fact, it depicts a scene that does not appear onstage, but artists often concentrated on a pivotal scene, even if it was not depicted onstage. On 'Pots and Plays', see Taplin (2007).
39 For a discussion of other productions of the same myth (both comic and satyric), see Chapter 4.
40 Seaford (1987, 142–3).
41 Aeschylus confirms this reading when Silenus later (v. 795) calls Prometheus a 'penis-loving child' (προσθοφιλὴς ὁ νεοσσός). Sophocles also uses this phallic pun in his *Dionysiskos* (*TrGF* 171), when Silenus paints a picture of his interactions with the newborn Dionysus: 'Whenever I bring him food and give it to him, he immediately feels my nose and brings his hands up to my bald head, laughing sweetly.'
42 On Odysseus' rhetorical prowess, see Worman (2002).
43 See Dunn's (2017, esp. 461) examination of 'Euripides and his Intellectual Context' for more on Polyphemus' oratorical style.
44 See Chapter 3 for further discussion of the sophistic elements of both Polyphemus and Odysseus.

45 See Whitmarsh (2016) on atheism in antiquity.

46 Seaford (1984, 174) helpfully scans the metre of the entire stasimon, as he does with all choral odes in the *Cyclops*.

47 Seaford (1984, 177) and O'Sullivan and Collard (2013, 178).

48 On the culinary skills of Polyphemus, see Chapter 4.

49 We cannot rule out that Euripides may have been imitating, or even parodying an earlier dramatist (Epicharmus, Aristias, Cratinus, or Callias) who staged this myth. See Chapter 4 for a more detailed discussion of previous theatrical productions of the myth.

50 Wine and sex overlap in the satyrs' ethos and in the similarity between πίνειν (to drink) and βινεῖν (to fuck). Cf. Lissarrague (1990a, 61).

51 Sutton (1980, 128). On Dionysiac poetics and Euripides' *Bacchae*, see Segal (1997). Cf. Mills (2006).

52 See Seaford (1984, 205).

53 Ambrose (1995-6) offers a full study of 'Ganymede in Euripides' *Cyclops*'.

54 Although Euripides' *Helen* presents a chorus that leaves the stage, Marshall (2014, 28-30) and others show that this is an anomaly, with most choruses discussing the prospect of leaving the stage, but ultimately rejecting the move. By actually going offstage, the chorus of the *Helen* surprises the audience by breaking convention.

55 The text here is unclear. See Seaford (1984, 221-2) and O'Sullivan and Collard (2013, 221).

56 Silenus speaks no further lines after he goes into the cave at v. 589.

Chapter 3

1 Momigliano (1929, 156), in his assessment of the *Cyclops*, says that Homer's material perishes in the hands of Euripides, but Seaford (1984, 51-9) shows that 'the major discrepancies can be assigned to the differences of (a) medium, (b) intellectual and social environment, and (c) genre'. See also Wetzel (1965), Katsouris (1997), Napolitano (2003), and Hunter (2009, 53-77) on Euripides' adaptation of the original.

2   For a broader discussion of 'Choric Self-Referentiality in Greek Tragedy' and its relationship to Dionysus, see Henrichs (1995).

3   The ithyphallic nature of the satyrs may also be related to Dionysus and the Dionysiac phallophoria at the City Dionysia. See Figure 1.3. Cf. Csapo and Slater (1995, 92–3).

4   Seaford (1981) treats the *Cyclops* in his study of 'Dionysiac drama and the Dionysiac mysteries', and Easterling (1997b) presents a compelling study of satyr drama's importance as 'A Show for Dionysus'.

5   I include the textually corrupt v. 73.

6   On the 'Form and Structure' of Euripidean drama (including the characteristic prologue), see Dubischar (2017, 367–89).

7   Torrance (2013, 251).

8   Rossi (1971) paints a vivid picture of Polyphemus as an unsuccessful komast. Hamilton (1979) looks broadly at the sympotic behaviour in which Polyphemus attempts to participate.

9   This is much like the satyrs, who are bestial slaves of Dionysus. On the slavish qualities of satyrs, see Griffith (2002).

10 Nikolsky (2011) details 'Slavery and Freedom in Euripides' *Cyclops*'.

11 On Dionysus and Euripides' *Bacchae*, see Seaford (1981), Segal (1997), and Mills (2006).

12 To understand the *Cyclops'* religious function, we can also turn to Sophocles' *Ichneutae* (*Trackers*), the satyr play for which we have the most verses (after the *Cyclops*). Even though Silenus and the satyrs appear to be attempting an escape from their slavery to Dionysus, neither the introduction nor the conclusion are extant, and I suspect that if they existed, we would see a serious change of heart before the play's end. The satyrs, who are the willing slaves of Dionysus, have a falling out with the god and attempt a new life without him (serving Apollo instead), but they realize the severity of their mistake and happily resume their position as slaves of Dionysus, where they once again sing, dance, and revel with the god. See Lloyd-Jones (2003) and Seidensticker (2012) for a more detailed examination of *Trackers*. Aeschylus' *Theoroi* or *Isthmiastae* (*TrGF* 3 F. 78a–82) also presents a

scenario in which the satyrs abandon Dionysus and are (presumably—we do not have the ending) reunited with the god at the end.

13 The only known exception to this rule is Euripides' *Alcestis*, which was apparently composed without a chorus of satyrs due to a particular Athenian decree just prior to the play's performance in 438. On this issue, see Chapter 4. It is interesting to note that satyrs were sometimes used as a chorus in comedy, but this appears to have been, at least at first, inspired by Euripides' unprecedented satyr-less satyr play. See Shaw (2014, 94–104) for a full discussion with relevant bibliography.

14 Hunter (2009).

15 See Chapter 1. On the meta-performative elements of satyr drama, see Griffith (2013).

16 Compare this passage to the similarly culinary parabasis in Metagenes' *Lover of Sacrifices* (K-A 15).

17 Cf. Kaimio (2001) and Torrance (2013).

18 Cf. Torrance (2013, 246).

19 O'Sullivan and Collard (2013, 28–39) offer a helpful overview of the various typical plots of satyr drama, along with relevant bibliography.

20 Sutton (1980, 140) suggests that Silenus was sometimes the coryphaeus (the chorus leader) rather than a separate actor, a choice that would free up space for a third character in the play that was not the elderly satyr. The Pronomos Vase inspired this argument because it presents eleven satyrs plus Silenus. However, it is more likely that this was the artist's choice rather than an actual record of the choreuts, since at this point in the theatre, there were fifteen chorus members rather than twelve. Regardless, Silenus would have been present, it seems, in every satyr play. On the three actor 'rule' and its effects, see Halleran (2005, 172–3). On the Pronomos Vase and its choreuts, see Griffith (2010, 47).

21 According to myth (cf. Pseudo-Hyginus, *Fabulae* 129), Dionysus visited the house of Oeneus, king of Calydon, and had a liaison with his wife, Althaea ('Healer').

22 There are many ancient sources for the *sikinnis*, but Aristoxenus (frr. 104, 106 Wehrli) puts it most succinctly, when he states that the *sikinnis* was the distinctive dance of satyr drama.

23 Festa (1918, esp. 51–70). Cf. Seidensticker (2010).

24 On the *kômos* and satyr drama, see Shaw (2014, 26–43). For *kômos* in Euripides' *Cyclops*, see Rossi (1971).

25 There has been a significant recent interest in komasts and dithyramb. Csapo and Miller's Introduction (2007) to *The Origins of Theater in Ancient Greece and Beyond: From Ritual to Drama* and Steinhart (2007) are particularly informative.

26 Cf. Smith (2007, 49–54) and Csapo and Miller (2007, 21).

27 On the similar function of satyrs and komasts, see Carpenter (2007, 43), Green (2007, 104–5), and Isler-Kerényi (2007, 91).

28 As we will see in the next chapter, Euripides also seems to connect his exploration of the *kômos* with the etymology and literary history of comedy.

29 These figures exclude both the *Rhesus* because its authorship is uncertain and *Alcestis* because it was staged in the fourth place of a tetralogy but does not use a satyr chorus. On the importance of the term *kômos* in *Alcestis*, see Chapter 4.

30 Henrichs (1984, quote on 206) presents a fruitful examination of the 'complexity and polymorphous nature of Dionysus' in relation to 'Loss of Self, Suffering, and Violence', using modern interpretations to shed light on Dionysus and his victims.

31 For recent studies of meta-poetry in Euripides' *Cyclops*, see Kaimio (2001) and Torrance (2013, 245–64).

32 The icon representing Dionysus Eleuthereus was a masked wooden phallus that was paraded from outside the city to the theatre for the festival. Cf. Csapo and Slater (1995, 104–6).

33 Cf. Bierl (2001, 79).

34 This reinforces the typical mythology of Dionysus, where the god's willing worshippers are rewarded, but his enemies are forced to be initiated and then punished with physical injury or death. See especially Euripides' *Bacchae*.

35 There was a tradition by Euripides' time of analysing Homer's epics
    allegorically. In fact, Socrates' student (and Euripides' contemporary)
    Antisthenes (445–365) composed a work entitled 'On the Use of Wine
    or On Drunkenness or On the Cyclops', a study that is now lost, but
    clearly used the story of the Cyclops as a broader allegory for wine
    consumption. Cf. Hunter (2009, 55).

36 There is a massive bibliography on *xenia*, especially its role in Homer's
    Odyssey. For helpful background, see Podlecki (1961), Donlan (1982),
    Herman (1987), Reece (1993), and Saïd (2011). On *xenia* in Euripides'
    Cyclops, see Konstan (1997, 24–42).

37 Homer, *Odyssey* 9.369.

38 Dougherty (2001, 136–7) notes that the most significant distinction
    between 'civilized' Greek and barbarian foreigner in the *Odyssey* is
    cannibalism.

39 Konstan (1990) provides a valuable discussion of the excesses of
    self-sufficiency in his 'Anthropology of Euripides' *Kyklops*'. See
    O'Sullivan (2012) on 'Dionysus, Polyphemos, and the Idea of Sicily in
    Euripides' *Cyclops*'.

40 On Polyphemus as a 'Sophisticated Cyclops' (and the problems with
    these associations), see Marshall (2005).

41 Cf. Hamilton (1979) and Seaford (1984, 52). On the connections
    between Polyphemus' cooking and his oratorical prowess, see Worman
    (2008, 121–52).

42 When recounting the story, Odysseus even notes (9.209) that the
    Cyclopes' wine was so potent that twenty parts of water should have
    been mixed into it.

43 For a similarly sympathetic reading of Polyphemus' character, see
    Arrowsmith's (1959) introduction to his translation of the play.

44 In fact, Odysseus comes and goes from the cave rather freely, leaving
    twice without Polyphemus' permission (375 and 625).

45 On Odysseus' sophistic elements, see Arrowsmith (1959, 2–8),
    Dougherty (1999), Worman (2002). Cf. Paganelli (1979), who looks at
    historical and political echoes in Euripides' *Cyclops* more broadly.

46   Steffen (1971, 206–11), Arnott (1972), and Worman (2002, 103 and
     119–21). O'Sullivan (2005) paints a powerful picture of the connections
     between Polyphemus and tyrants, suggesting that the Cyclops should
     not particularly be associated with sophists, but this connection to
     tyrants does not, I think, diminish the philosophical associations of the
     monster.

47   See Worman (2002) for a helpful study of 'Euripides, Ingestive
     Rhetoric, and Euripides' *Cyclops*'.

48   As Hunter (2009, 76) points out, there is also a potential contact to
     Hesiod's *Works and Days*, 209–10, where a hawk talks to a nightingale:
     'I shall make you my dinner if I wish, or I shall let you go. Stupid
     is he who would wish to contend against those stronger than he is:
     for he is deprived of the victory, and suffers pains in addition to his
     humiliations.' Trans. Most (2007).

49   Hunter (2009, 67). It is interesting to note that the same comments
     could be made about the satyrs. See Chapter 1 for more on the
     ambiguities of satyrs.

50   On Euripides and sophism generally, see Conacher (1998). On the
     Cyclops and sophism, see Paganelli (1979, 19–60) and O'Sullivan
     (2005).

51   Goins (1991) presents a full study of 'The Heroism of Odysseus in
     Euripides' *Cyclops*'.

52   It is arguable that Zeus did not drive Odysseus and his men to the
     island of the Cyclopes in the *Odyssey*, since Odysseus chose to visit
     the island after Zeus blew him off course to the island across from the
     Cyclopes. Either way, however, the divine intervention is elided.

53   On the sophistic interest in explaining the natural world without
     resorting to mythology and divinity, see Rubel (2014, 18–22).
     Whitmarsh (2016, 75–144) offers a complete study of atheism in
     Classical Athens, including a good deal on the sophistic movement.

54   Straus Clay (1983) provides the seminal study of 'Gods and Men in the
     Odyssey'.

55   In fact, one of the most perplexing moments in the *Odyssey* is found just
     after Odysseus escapes the island of the Cyclopes and sacrifices a ram to

Zeus in hopes of arriving home safely, but Zeus rejects the offering and plans a way to destroy Odysseus' ships and comrades (9.551–5).

56 O'Sullivan and Collard (2013, 51).

57 Hunter (2009, 64).

58 See Paganelli (1979) and Hunter (2009).

59 On the Athenian Empire, see Rhodes (1985).

60 See book 6 of Thucydides' *History of the Peloponnesian War* for a primary source narrative. Cf. Kagan (1981) for details on the Sicilian Expedition in particular.

61 Plutarch *Life of Nicias* 29.3–5.

62 Plutarch *Life of Nicias* 29.2–4.

63 See, for example, Kagan (1987).

64 It is possible, perhaps even likely, that earlier playwrights had also situated their stories of Odysseus and the Cyclops in Sicily, but we cannot know for sure. See Chapter 4 for more on preceding theatrical versions of the myth. For more on the cultural importance of Sicily in Greece, see Willi (2008).

65 This assumes, of course, that Euripides staged his play at some point between 412 and 408, which is the scholarly consensus. See Chapter 4 for a more complete discussion of the date of the *Cyclops*.

66 For an examination of 'Thucydides' Ignorant Athenians and the Drama of the Sicilian Expedition', see Smith (2004).

67 Torrance (2013, 263).

68 Lissarrague (1990b, 236).

Chapter 4

1 For a useful collection of essays on the reception of Greek drama, see van Zyl Smit (2016).

2 It is also unique in that it is one of only two extant plays (along with the dubiously attributed *Rhesus*) that treats events from Homeric epic.

3 Beta (2015) provides a valuable study of the reception of Euripides' *Cyclops*. He notes (2015, 608) that the 'singing Cyclops invented by

Euripides probably inspired the equally singing Cyclopes we find in other [later] Greek authors', but even this is uncertain. The first published edition of the *Cyclops* was published in 1503 by Aldo Manuzio, edited by Johannes Gregoropoulos, but it remained relatively unpopular/unknown until Casaubon (1605) wrote a scholarly treatise differentiating Greek satyr plays and Roman satire. In 1819, Percy Bysshe Shelley translated the *Cyclops* into English, and the famous early twentieth-century Dutch composer Willem Pijper co-produced *De Cycloop* with Balthazar Verhagen. More recently, Rush Rehm staged *Cyclops (Nobody's Musical)* at Stanford University in 1983, and Jayson Landon Marcus adapted Shelly's translation into *Cyclops (A Rock Opera)* in 2011 for staging in Los Angeles and New York. For discussion of Italian, German, Modern Greek, and Czech productions of the *Cyclops* (most of which exhibit experimental, 'Euripidean' qualities), see Beta (2015, 613–17).

4   Shaw (2014, 26–55).

5   For a full exploration of these philosopher's connections, both explicit and implicit, see Shaw (2014, 13–25).

6   The Suda (chi 318; K-A, Chionides T1) states that Chionides was the first to compete in Old Comedy at the City Dionysia with a production in 486, which matches evidence on the Athenian victory lists (*IG* II² 2325). Rusten (2006) provides one of the most useful recent discussions on the origins of comedy.

7   See Csapo and Miller's introduction (2007, 12), which also supplies a useful bibliography.

8   Cf. Leonhardt (1991), Steinhart (2007, 212), and Shaw (2014, 31–2).

9   Hedreen (2004) offers a study on this famous myth in early performative contexts.

10   Fifteen examples are extant: *ARV*² 1031, no. 40; *ARV*² 1041, no. 1; *ARV*² 1055, no. 76, 1630; *ARV*² 1269, no. 3; *ARV*² 120, no. 17; *ARV*² 688; *ARV*² 1253, no. 57; *ARV*² 1247, no. 1; *ARV*² 1249, no. 12; *ARV*² 1188, no. 1; Tillyard 1923, p. 85, no. 141; *ARV*² 1153, no. 13; *ARV*² 1154, no. 29; *ARV*² 1155, no. 6; *ARV*² 1152, no. 8.

11 On Arion and dithyramb, see Csapo (2003). Shaw (forthcoming) uses Arion's myth to examine the connections between 'Satyrs, Dolphins, Dithyramb and Drama'.

12 This connection seems to be based more in performance than mythology. For a discussion of satyrs and komasts, see Csapo and Miller (2007, 12–24), Isler-Kerényi (2007), and Shaw (2014, 33–9).

13 Seaford (1984, 10–12).

14 Shaw (2014).

15 Arnott (1972) provides a sustained study of parody in Euripides' *Cyclops*. On humorous diction in satyr drama, including *Cyclops*, see: Redondo (2003, 413–31), López Eire (2003, 387–412), and Slenders (2005, 39–52). Voelke (2001, 95–108), like Seaford (1987, 142–3), provides a study of obscenity in satyr plays that concentrates on a frequently employed *phalakron* ('bald head') joke.

16 Seaford (1977, 84; 1984, 92).

17 Silenus uses sexual innuendo at the end of four verses (δέμας, v. 2; δορός, v. 5; δορί, v. 7; δόρυ, v. 15). Cf. Harrison (2005a).

18 LSJ *ad. loc.*

19 Cf. examples from Old Comedy (e.g. Aristophanes, *Wasps* 1062, and *Lysistrata* 863 and 937), in which the demonstrative τοῦτο clearly indicates the comic phallus.

20 Seaford (1984, 139) provides a nuanced reading of the remainder of the passage, which becomes less explicitly sexual but more implicitly obscene. In particular, he argues that αὐχήν (neck) 'may contain the *double entendre* penis'. After mentioning Helen's fondness for multiple partners, the chorus launches into a description of Alexander, mentioning his midsection (μέσον), which may also be used sexually. Even the term for his multicoloured pants (θυλάκους) has the meaning sack and, euphemistically, scrotum.

21 Seaford (1984, 187). Cf. Sophron 25, where the female genitalia are 'widowed' and Aristophanes *Lysistrata* 956, where the penis is 'orphaned'.

22 For an excellent discussion of the play and the following issue, see
    Slater (2005, 2013). On *Alcestis'* similarities to satyr drama, see Sutton
    (1980, 180–92) and Parker (2007).

23 Scholiast to *Acharnians* 67. Freedom of speech in the theatre was an
    issue that Athenians wrestled with regularly in their democracy. On the
    decree and this type of legislation more generally, see Halliwell (1984
    and 1991), Sommerstein (1986), and Henderson (1998).

24 Callias staged his comedy *Satyroi* the following year, presumably
    in response to Euripides' satyr-less *Alcestis*. *IG Urb. Rom.* 216.4: ἐπὶ
    θεοδώρου [438/7] Σατύροις.

25 See Chapter 1 for discussion of post-classical satyr drama, which did
    take aim at contemporary philosophers and political figures.

26 Marshall (2000).

27 Shaw (2014, 99–105).

28 Wright (2012) presents an excellent study on competitive poetics in
    comedy.

29 For a helpful study of comedy's use of tragedy in particular, see Farmer
    (2017).

30 Cf. Hunter (2009, 55). See Chapter 3.

31 This point holds extra significance when considered alongside the
    competitive nature of ancient theatrical performance. Not only was the
    Cyclops performed in a tetralogy against two rival tragedians, but it was
    the last performance viewed before judging took place.

32 As Mark Griffith (2002, 212) notes, the satyrs have a 'timeless and
    unchanging quality' and 'are always the "same" satyrs, who always
    were and always will be getting into and out of trouble, then and
    now'.

33 On the connections between Euripides' *Cyclops* and Homer's original,
    see Ferante (1960), Sutton (1974), Seaford (1984, 51–9), Katsouris
    (1997), Napolitano (2003, 1–25), and Hunter (2009, 53–77). Most
    scholars believe that Euripides offers a fairly faithful theatrical
    adaptation of book nine of the *Odyssey*. See especially Wetzel (1965),
    who at the end of his study, even presents a table of Euripidean verses
    that he believes are drawn from the epic original.

34 Napolitano (2005). Cf. Hunter (2009, 56): the *Cyclops* 'does not merely "translate" the model into its own idiom and linguistic form but also offers one or more exegetical readings of that model'.

35 Much of the following discussion is inspired by Hunter's (2009, 53–77) outstanding analysis of the literary relationship between Homer's *Odyssey* and Euripides' *Cyclops*.

36 Hunter (2009, 60).

37 Lissarrague (1990b, 236).

38 This term is the traditional name for Aesop's fables. Cf. Wright (2006, 34) and Hunter (2009).

39 See, for example, Herodotus' *Histories* 1.4.2.

40 Wright (2006, 36). Cf. Guthrie (1971, 27–34).

41 See Chapter 3.

42 Matthew Wright (2006) and Richard Hunter (2009) have provided fruitful discussions of the characters' seeming knowledge of their own (and each other's) mythological history.

43 Pindar (*Olympian* 1.27–9) is the earliest example of a poet using the term 'mythos' with the sense that a story should not be believed.

44 Cf. Lucian's *True Histories* 1.3.

45 Jaillard (2011, 133–50) provides an interpretive essay on the *Homeric Hymn to Dionysus*, including (143–4) a brief look at some of its differences with Euripides' *Cyclops*.

46 Olson (1988).

47 See, for example, K-A Testimonia 1, 4, 6, 7. On Epicharmus generally, see Rodríguez-Noriega Guillén (1996), Willi (2008), and Bosher (2014).

48 Aristotle, *Poetics* 1448a. Aristotle's remarks are supported by Diogenes Laertius' account (K-A T9) that Epicharmus lived to the age of ninety and Lucian's comment (K-A T9) that he lived to ninety-seven. Cf. Pickard-Cambridge (1962, 232–5).

49 *TrGF* T7.

50 On the 'Euripidean Biography', see Scodel (2017).

51 Cf. Rusten (2011, 58), who notes the 'apparent lack of a chorus'. Shaw (2014, 68–71) outlines the reasons to believe Epicharmus (at least on occasion) used a chorus.

52 K-A 11 (*Harpagae*) and K-A 65 (*Heracles and the Girdle*) refer to Sicily and Aetna respectively, and *Odysseus Nauagos* and *Alcyoneus* mention the famous Sicilian shepherd and inventor of pastoral poetry, Diomus.

53 We do not know where Epicharmus (or Aristias, Cratinus, or Callias for that matter) situated his play, but Euripides' choice may have been an homage of sorts to the comic dramatist's earlier version of the story. It is also possible that the Sicilian location may have passed into myth by this point. Cf. Thucydides' *History* 6.2.

54 Seaford (1984, 52). Cf. Hamilton (1979).

55 Cf. Katsouris (1997).

56 Cratinus' play is dated to the 430s. Otherwise, the plays were not particularly similar, since Cratinus' *Odysseis* involved a massive scene change, depicting both ship and shipwreck onstage. Cf. Bakola (2010, 234–46). For a study of Cratinus' and Euripides' plays, see Kaibel (1895) and Tanner (1915).

57 See Davidson (1997) and Shaw (2014a).

58 See Nesselrath (1990, 234) on comedy's interest in the kottabos.

59 The primary source of these fragments, Athenaeus' late second-, early third-century CE *Deipnosophistae*, somewhat taints these conclusions, though, since it is a fictional dialogue on food and drink that quotes a vast range of literary and historical sources.

60 For more on 'Euripides' Cyclopean Symposium', see Hamilton (1979). On the implied sexual encounter, see Fletcher (2005).

61 On Sophocles' *Philoctetes*, see Roisman's (2005) study in this same series.

62 Seaford (1984, 112) suggests ἀμφίθυρον as a potential textual emendation at *Cyclops* 60 for the corrupt ἀμφιβαίνεις.

63 Katsouris (1997, 23–4) notes that this is a 'Sophoclean reminiscence … which does not have any theatrical significance'.

64 Cf. Davidson (1990).

65 Marshall (2005, 109).

66 As Podlecki (2009, 77) notes, Euripides' *Andromeda* 'seems to have created a sensation' after it was staged in 412.

67 Austin and Olson (2004) provide the most recent commentary on Aristophanes' *Thesmophoriazusae*. For the play's interaction with *Andromeda*, see xxxiii–iv and 311–32.

68 For a quick overview of the *Cyclops'* relation to Aristophanes' *Thesmophoriazusae*, see Austin and Olson (2004, lxiii–iv).

69 Torrance (2013, 296).

70 Cf. Seaford (1982, 170).

71 Wright (2005).

72 Griffith (2002, 206–7).

73 Other trilogies/tetralogies connected by plot include (in roughly chronological order): Aeschylus' *Phineus, Persians, Glaucus Pontius,* and satyric *Prometheus*; Aeschylus' *Laius, Oedipus, Seven Against Thebes, Sphinx*; Aristias' *Perseus, Tantalus,* and satyric *Wrestlers* (fourth play unknown); Polyphrasmon's *Lycurgeia*; Aeschylus' *Suppliant Women, Egyptians, Danaids, Amymone*; Aeschylus' *Edonians, Bassarids, Youths, Lycurgus*; Philocles' *Pandionis*; Sophocles' *Telepheia*; Euripides' *Cretan Women, Alcmaeon in Psophis, Telephus, Alcestis*; Euripides' *Medea, Philoctetes, Dictys, Reapers*; Xenocles' *Oedipus, Lycaon, Bacchae, Athamas*; Euripides' *Alexandros, Palamedes, Trojan Women, Sisyphus*; Euripides' *Oenomaus, Chrysippus, Phoenissae* (satyr play unknown); Euripides' *Iphigenia at Aulis, Alcmaeon, Bacchae* (satyr play unknown); Meletus' *Oedipodeia*.

74 O'Sullivan and Collard (2013, 40) argue that 'such parallels do not … constitute dating criteria'. While it is true that one can find many overlapping themes within Euripides' corpus, it is also true that such themes across a tetralogy would be appealing. Ultimately, though, there is too little information to date with certainty.

75 This concurs with Ion of Chios' comment, in Plutarch's *Life of Pericles* 5, that 'virtue, like the tragic production, should not be without a satyric element'.

76 Euripides' *Helen* and *Andromeda* were definitely performed in 412, while the date of *Iphigenia among the Taurians* is uncertain.

77 Wright (2006). For more on dating, see Chapter 1.

78 Euripides' *Cyclops* vv. 20, 62, 95, 106, 114, 130, 298, 366, 395, 599, 660, and 703.

79 For an interesting, though theoretical, study of how Aeschylus' satyric *Proteus* engaged with the *Oresteia* (the extant trilogy of tragedies made up of *Agamemnon*, *Libation Bearers*, and *Eumenides*), see Griffith (2002).

80 See Seaford (1982, 168–72).

81 Parry (1930, 140–1) suggests that Euripides' *Cyclops* was staged in 409 and that the playwright was responding to Aristophanes' lampoon of the *Andromeda*.

Bibliography

Ambrose, Z. P. 1995–1996. 'Ganymede in Euripides' Cyclops: A Study in Homosexuality and Misogyny', *NECJ* 23: 91–95.

Ambrose, Z. P. 2005. 'Family Loyalty and Betrayal in Euripides' *Cyclops* and *Alcestis*: A Recurrent Theme in Satyr Play', in Harrison 2005b, 21–38.

Arnott, G. 1972. 'Parody and Ambiguity in Euripides' *Cyclops*', in *Antidosis. Festschrift für Walther Kraus zum 70*, ed. R. Hanslik, A. Lesky, and H. Schwabl, 21–30. Vienna.

Arrowsmith, W. 1959. 'Introduction to *Cyclops*', in *The Complete Greek Tragedies*, vol. 3, 224–30. Chicago. (Reprinted in Seidensticker, 1989: 179–87).

Austin, C. and D. Olson. 2004. *Aristophanes Thesmophoriazusae*. Oxford.

Bakola, E. 2005. '*Old Comedy Disguised as Satyr-Play: A New Reading of Cratinus'* Dionysalexandros (P. Oxy. 663)', *Zeitschrift für Papyrologie und Epigraphik* 154: 46–58.

Bakola, E. 2010. *Cratinus and the Art of Comedy*. Oxford.

Beta, S. 2015. 'Cyclops', in *Brill's Companion to the Reception of Euripides*, ed. R. Lauriola and K. Demetriou, 605–19. Leiden.

Biehl, W. 1986. *Euripides Kyklops*. Heidelberg.

Bierl, A. 2001. *Der Chor in der alten Komödie. Ritual und Performativität*. Munich/Leipzig.

Bierl, A. 2006. 'Tragödie als Spiel und das Satyrspiel: Die Geburt des griechischen Theaters aus dem Geiste des Chortanzes und seines Gottes Dionysos', in *Kind und Spiel*, ed. J. Sánchez de Murillo and M. Thurner, 111–38. Stuttgart.

Bosher, K. 2014. 'Epicharmus and Early Sicilian Comedy', in *Cambridge Companion to Greek Comedy*, ed. M. Revermann, 79–94. Cambridge.

Brommer, F. 1937. *Satyroi*. Würzburg.

Burkert, W. 1966. 'Greek Tragedy and Sacrificial Ritual', *Greek, Roman, and Byzantine Studies* 7: 87–121.

Burkert, W. 1985. *Greek Religion*. Trans. John Raffan. Cambridge, MA.

Carpenter, T. H. 2005. 'Images of Satyr Plays in South "Italy", in Harrison 2005, 219–36.

Carpenter, T. H. 2007. '"Introduction" and "Discussion" to "Komasts and Predramatic Ritual"', in Csapo and Miller 2007, 41–47 and 108–17.

Casaubon, I. 1605. *De satyrica Graecorum poesi et Romanorum satira libri duo*. (Facsimile with introduction by Peter E. Medine, 1973: Delmar, N.Y.). Paris.

Cipolla, P. 2003. *Poeti Minori del Dramma Satiresco, Testo Critico, Traduzione e Commento*. Amsterdam.

Collard, C. 1970. 'On the Tragedian Chairemon', *Journal of Hellenic Studies* 90: 22–34.

Collard, C. and M. Cropp. 2008. *Euripides Fragments*. Cambridge, MA.

Conacher, D. J. 1998. *Euripides and the Sophists*. London.

Conrad, G. 1997. *Der Silen*. Trier.

Cozzoli, A.-T. 2003. 'Sositeo e il nuova dramma satiresco', in Martina 2003, 265–91.

Csapo, E. 2003. 'The Dolphins of Dionysus', in *Poetry, Theory, Praxis*, ed. E. Csapo and M. C. Miller, 69–98. Oxford.

Csapo, E. 2007. 'The Men Who Built the Theatres: *Theatropolitai, Theatronai and Arkhitektones*', in Wilson 2007, 87–121.

Csapo, E. 2010. *Actors and Icons of the Ancient Theater*. Malden, MA and Oxford.

Csapo, E. and M. Miller. 2007. *The Origins of Theater in Ancient Greece and Beyond: From Ritual to Drama*. Cambridge.

Csapo, E. and W. J. Slater. 1995. *The Context of Ancient Drama*. Ann Arbor, MI.

Dale, A. M. 1969. *Collected Papers*. Cambridge.

Davidson, J. 1990. 'The Cave of Philoctetes', *Mnemosyne* 43: 307–15.

Davidson, J. 1997. *Courtesans and Fishcakes*. London.

Depew, D. 2007. 'From Hymn to Tragedy: Aristotle's Genealogy of Poetic Kinds', in Csapo and Miller 2007, 126–49.

di Marco, M. 'L'ambiguo statuto del dramma satiresco', in *Letteratura e riflessione sulla letteratura nella cultura classica*, ed. G. Arrighetti.

Donlan, W. 1982. 'Reciprocities in Homer', *CW* 75: 137–75.

Dougherty, C. 2001. *The Raft of Odysseus: The Ethnographic Imagination of Homer's Odyssey*. Oxford.

Dubischar, D. 2017. 'Form and Structure', in McClure 2017, 367–89.

Duchemin, J. 1945. *Le Cyclope, édition critique et commentée*. Paris.

Dunn, F. M. 2017. 'Euripides in his Intellectual Context', in McClure 2017, 447–67.

Easterling, P. E. 1997a. *The Cambridge Companion to Greek Tragedy*. Cambridge.

Easterling, P. E. 1997b. 'A Show for Dionysus', in Easterling 1997a, 36–53.

Farmer, M. C. 2017. *Tragedy on the Comic Stage*. Oxford.

Ferante, D. 1960. 'Il *Ciclope* di Euripide ed il IX dell' Odissea', *Dioniso* 34: 165–81.

Festa, V. 1918. 'Sikinnis', *Memorie della Reale Accademia di Archeologia* 3: 37–74.

Fletcher, J. 2005. 'Perjury and the Perversion of Language in Euripides' *Cyclops*', in Harrison 2005b, 53–66.

Foley, H. P. 2014. 'Performing Gender in Greek Old and New Comedy', in Revermann 2014, 259–74.

Fraser, P. M. 1972. *Ptolemaic Alexandria*, 2 vols. Oxford.

Gantz, T. 1993. *Early Greek Myth: A Guide to Literary and Artistic Sources*, vol. 1. Baltimore.

Gibert, J. 2002. 'Recent Work on Greek Satyr-Play', *Classical Journal* 87: 79–88.

Goins, S. 1991. 'The Heroism of Odysseus in Euripides' *Cyclops*', *Eos* 79: 187–94.

Goldhill, S. 1997 'The Language of Tragedy: Rhetoric and Communication', in Easterling 1997a, 127–50.

Green, J. R. 2007. 'Let's Hear It for the Fat Man: Padded Dancers and the Prehistory of Drama', in Csapo and Miller 2007, 96–107.

Green, J. R., and E. W. Handley. 1995. *Images of the Greek Theater*. London.

Griffith, M. 2002. 'Slaves of Dionysos: Satyrs, Audience, and the Ends of the *Oresteia*', *Classical Antiquity* 21: 195–258.

Griffith, M. 2005. 'Satyrs, Citizens, and Self-Presentation', in Harrison 2005b, 161–99.

Griffith, M. 2006. 'Sophocles' Satyr-Plays and the Language of Romance', in *Sophocles and the Greek Language*, ed. I. De Jong and A. Rijksbaro, 51–72. Leiden.

Griffith, M. 2008. 'Greek middle-brow drama (Something to do with Aphrodite?)', in Revermann and Wilson 2008, 59–87.

Griffith, M. 2010. 'Satyr-play and tragedy face to face, from East to West', in Taplin and Wyles 2010, 47–63.

Griffith, M. 2013. 'Satyr-play, dithyramb, and the geo-politics of Dionysian style in fifth-century Athens', in Kowalzig and Wilson 2013, 257–81.

Griffith, M. 2015. *Greek Satyr Play: Five Studies*. Berkeley, CA.

Guthrie, W. K. C. 1962–1981. *A History of Greek Philosophy*, 6 vols. Cambridge.

Hall, E. 1998. 'Ithyphallic Males Behaving Badly: Or, Satyr Drama as Gendered Tragic Ending', in *Parchments of Gender: Deciphering the Bodies of Antiquity*, ed. M. Wyke, 13–37. Oxford.

Hall, E. 2006. *The Theatrical Cast of Athens. Interactions between Ancient Greek Drama and Society*. Oxford.

Halleran, M. R. 2005. 'Episodes', in *A Companion to Greek Tragedy*, ed. J. Gregory, 167–82. Oxford.

Halliwell, S. 1984. 'Ancient interpretations of ὀνομαστὶ κωμῳδεῖν in Aristophanes', *Classical Quarterly* 34: 83–88.

Halliwell, S. 1991. 'Uses of laughter in Greek Culture', *Classical Quarterly* 41: 279–96.

Halliwell, S., et al. 1995. *Aristotle: Poetics; Longinus: On the Sublime; Demetrius: On Style*. Cambridge, MA.

Hamilton, R. 1979. 'Euripides' Cyclopean Symposium', *Phoenix* 33: 287–92.

Harrison, G. W. M. 2005a. 'Positioning of satyr drama and characterization in the *Cyclops*', in Harrison 2005b, 237–58.

Harrison, G. W. M. (ed.). 2005b. *Satyr Drama: Tragedy at Play*. Swansea.

Harrison, G. W. M. and V. Liapis. 2013. *Performance in Greek and Roman Theatre*. Leiden.

Harrison, T. 1990. *The Trackers of Oxyrhynchus. The Delphi Text 1988*. London.

Hedreen, G. M. 1992. *Silens in Attic Black-Figure Vase Painting: Myth and Performance*. Ann Arbor, MI.

Hedreen, G. M. 2004. 'The Return of Hephaistos, Dionysiac Processional Ritual and the Creation of a Visual Narrative', *Journal of Hellenic Studies* 124: 38–64.

Hedreen, G. M. 2007. 'Myths and Rituals in Athenian Vase Paintings of Silens', in Csapo and Miller 2007, 150–95.

Henderson, J. 1998. 'Attic Old Comedy, Frank Speech, and Democracy', in *Democracy, Empire, and the Arts in Fifth-Century Athens*, ed. D. Boedeker and K. A. Raaflaub, 255–73. Cambridge, MA.

Henderson, J. 2000. *Birds, Lysistrata, Women at the Thesmophoria*. Cambridge, MA.

Henrichs, A. 1984. 'Loss of Self, Suffering, and Violence: The modern view of Dionysus from Nietzsche to Girard', *HSCP* 88: 205–40.

Henrichs, A. 1995. '"Why Should I Dance?" Choric Self-Referentiality in Greek Tragedy', *Arion* 3: 56–111.

Herington, C. J. 1985. *Poetry into Drama*. Berkeley, CA.

Herman, G. 1987. *Ritualized Friendship and the Greek City*. Cambridge.

Hunter, R. 2009. *Critical Moments in Classical Literature: Studies in the Ancient View of Literature and its Uses*. Cambridge.

Ieranò, G. 1997. *Il ditirambo di Dioniso: le testimonianze antiche*. Pisa.

Isler-Kerényi, C. 2007. 'Komasts, Mythic Imaginary, and Ritual', in Csapo and Miller 2007, 77–95.

Jaillard, D. 2011. 'The Seventh Homeric Hymn: An Epiphanic Sketch', in *The Homeric Hymns: Interpretative Essays*, ed. A. Faulkner, 133–50. Oxford.

Kagan, D. 1981. *The Peace of Nicias and the Sicilian Expedition*. Ithaca.

Kagan, D. 1987. *The Fall of the Athenian Empire*. Ithaca.

Kaibel, G. 1895. 'Kratinos' ΟΔΥΣΣΗΣ und Euripides' ΚΥΚΛΟΨ', *Hermes* 30: 71–89.

Kaimio, M. [et al.] 2001. 'Metatheatricality in the Greek Satyr-Play', *Arctos: Acta Philologica Fennica* 35: 35–78.

Katsouris, A. G. 1997. 'Euripides' *Cyclops* and Homer's *Odyssey*', *Prometheus* 13: 1–24.

Kerényi, C. 1996. *Dionysos: Archetypal Image of Indestructible Life*. Trans. Ralph Manheim. Princeton, NJ.

Keuls, E. 1993. *The Reign of the Phallus. Sexual Politics in Ancient Athens*. Berkeley, CA.

Konstan, D. 1990. 'An Anthropology of Euripides' *Kyklops*', in J. J. Winkler and F. I. Zeitlin 1990, 207–27.

Konstan, D. 1997. *Friendship in the Classical World*. Cambridge.

Kowalzig, B. and P. Wilson (eds.). 2013. *Dithyramb in Context*. Oxford.

Krumeich, R., N. Pechstein, and B. Seidensticker. 1999. *Das griechische Satyrspiel*. Darmstadt.

Lämmle, R. 2007. 'Der eingescholssene Dritte. Zur Funktion des Dionysos im Satyrspiel', in *Literatur und Religion 2. Wege zu einer mythischrituellen Poetik bei den Griechen*, ed. A. Bierl, R. Lämmle, and K. Wesselmann, 335–86. Berlin/New York.

Lämmle, R. 2013. *Poetik des Satyrspiels*. Heidelberg.

Lasserre, F. 1973. 'Le drame satyrique', *Rivista di filologia e di istruzione classica* 101: 273–301. (Reprinted in Seidensticker, 1989: 252–86).

Lawler, L. B. 1964. 'The Dance of the Satyr Play', in *The Dance of the Ancient Greek Theater*. Iowa.

Leonhardt, J. 1991. *Phalloslied und Dithyrambos: Aristoteles und Ursprung des Griechishcen Dramas*. Heidelberg.

Lissarrague, F. 1990. *The Aesthetics of the Greek Banquet*. Princeton, NJ.

Lissarrague, F. 1990a. 'The Sexual Life of Satyrs', in *Before Sexuality*, ed. D. M. Halperin, J. J. Winkler, and F. I. Zeitlin, 53–81. Princeton, NJ.

Lissarrague, F. 1990b. 'Why Satyrs Are Good to Represent', in J. J. Winkler and F. I. Zeitlin 1990, 228–36.

Lissarrague, F. 1993. 'On the Wildness of Satyrs', in *Masks of Dionysos*, ed. T. H. Carpenter and C. A. Faraone, 207–20. Ithaca.

Lloyd-Jones, H. 2003. *Sophocles Fragments*. Cambridge, MA.

López Eire, A. 2003. 'Tragedy and Satyr-Drama: Linguistic Criteria', in Sommerstein 2003, 387–412.

Lord, C. 1974. 'Aristotle's History of Poetry', *Transactions of the American Philological Association* 104: 195–229.

Marshall, C. W. 2000. '*Alcestis* and the Problem of Prosatyric Drama', *Classical Journal* 95: 229–38.

Marshall, C. W. 2001. 'The Consequences of Dating the Cyclops', in *In Altum: Seventy-Five Years of Classical Studies in Newfoundland*, 225–41. St. John's, Newfoundland.

Marshall, C. W. 2005. 'The sophisticated Cyclops', in G. W. M. Harrison 2005b, 103–17.

Marshall, C. W. 2014. *The Structure and Performance of Euripides' Helen*. Cambridge.

Martina, A. (ed.). 2003. *Teatro greco postclassico e teatro latino: teorie e prassi drammatica*. Rome.

Mathieson, T. J. 1999. *Apollo's Lyre: Greek Music and Music Theory in Antiquity and the Middle Ages*. Lincoln, NE.

McClure, L. K. (ed.). 2017. *A Companion to Euripides*. West Sussex.

Millis, W. and D. Olson. 2012. *Inscriptional Records for the Dramatic Festivals in Athens*. Leiden.

Mills, S. 2006. *Euripides: Bacchae*. London.

Momigliano, A. 1929. 'Rileggendo il 'Ciclope'', *Atene e Roma* 10: 154–60.

Morelli, G. 2001. *Teatro attico e pittura vascolare: una tragedia di Cheremone nella ceramic italiota*. Hildesheim.

Most, G. W. 2007. *Hesiod. Theogony, Works and Days, Testimonia*. Cambridge, MA.

Murray, A. T. (revised by G. E. Dimock). 1995. *Homer. Odyssey*. Cambridge, MA.

Nagy, G. 1990. *Pindar's Homer: The Lyric Possession of an Epic Past*. Baltimore, MD.

Nagy, G. 2007. 'Introduction and Discussion', in Csapo and Miller 2007, 121–25.

Napolitano, M. 2003. *Euripide. Il Ciclope*. Venice.

Napolitano, M. 2005. 'Appunti sullo statuto letterario del Ciclope di Euripide', *Dioniso* 4: 42–55.

Nesselrath, H. G. 1990. *Die Attische Mittlere Komödie*. Darmstadt.

Nicolucci, V. 2003. 'Il dramma satiresco alla corte di Attalo I', in Martina 2003, 325–42.

Nikolsky, B. 2011. 'Slavery and Freedom in Euripides' *Cyclops*', in *Reading Ancient Slavery*, ed. R. Alston, E. Hall, and L. Proffitt, 121–51. London.

Olson, D. 2006–2011. *Athenaeus: The Learned Banqueters*, vv. 1–7. Cambridge, MA.

Olson, S. D. 1988. 'Dionysus and the Pirates in Euripides' "Cyclops"', *Hermes* 116: 502–4.

O'Sullivan, P. 2005. 'Of Sophists, Tyrants, and Polyphemos: The Nature of the Beast in Euripides' *Cyclops*', in Harrison 2005b, 21–38.

O'Sullivan, P. 2012. 'Dionysos, Polyphemos, and the Idea of Sicily in Euripides' *Cyclops*', in *Greek Drama IV: Texts, Contexts, Performance*, ed. D. Rosenbloom and J. Davidson, 169–89. Oxford.

O'Sullivan, P. 2017. '*Cyclops*', in McClure 2017, 315–33.

O'Sullivan, P. and C. Collard 2013. *Euripides: Cyclops and Major Fragments of Greek Satyric Drama*. Warminster.

Paganelli, L. 1979. *Echi Storico-Politici nel 'Ciclope' Euripideo*. Padua.

Parker, L. P. E. 2007. *Euripides. Alcestis*. Edited with Introduction and Commentary. Oxford.

Parry, M. 1930. 'Studies in the technique of Oral Verse-Making, I: Homer and Homeric Style', *HSPC* 41: 73–147.

Pechstein, N. 1998. *Euripides Satyrographos: ein Kommentar zu den Euripideischen Satyrspielfragmenten*. Leipzig.

Pickard-Cambridge, A. W. 1962. *Dithyramb, Tragedy and Comedy* (Second Edition revised by T. B. L. Webster). Oxford.

Pickard-Cambridge, A. W. 1968. *Dramatic Festivals of Athens* (Second Edition revised by J. Gould and D. M. Lewis). Oxford.

Podlecki, A. J. 1961. 'Guest-Gifts and Nobodies in *Odyssey* 9', *Phoenix* 15: 125–33.

Podlecki, A. J. 2009. 'Echoes of the Prometheia in Euripides' *Andromeda*', in *The Play of Texts and Fragments*, ed. J. R. C. Cousland and J. R. Hume, 77–94. Leiden.

Pretagostini, R. 2003. 'La representazione dell' *Agên* e la nuova drammaturgia', in Martina 2003, 161–75.

Pritchard, D. 2004. 'Kleisthenes, Participation and the Dithyrambic Contests of Late Archaic and Classical Athens', *Phoenix* 58: 208–28.

Pucci, P. 1998. *The Song of the Sirens: Essays on Homer*. Lanham, MD.

Rankin, D. 2014. *Sophists, Socratics, and Cynics*. New York.

Redondo, J. 2003. 'Satyric Diction in the Extant Sophoclean Fragments: A Reconsideration', in Sommerstein 2003, 413–31.

Reece, S. 1993. *The Stranger's Welcome: Oral Theory and the Aesthetics of the Homeric Hospitality Scene*. Ann Arbor, MI.

Rehm, R. 2017. *Understanding Greek Tragic Theatre*. London and New York.

Revermann, M. 2013. 'Generalizing about Props: Greek Drama, Comparator Traditions, and the Analysis of Stage Objects', in Harrison and Liapis 2013, 77–88.

Revermann, M. (ed.). 2014. *The Cambridge Companion to Greek Comedy*. Cambridge.

Reynolds, L. D. and N. G. Wilson. 2014. *Scribes and Scholars: A Guide to the Transmission of Greek and Latin Literature*. Oxford.

Rhodes, P. J. 1985. *The Athenian Empire*. Oxford.

Rodríguez-Noriega Guillén, L. 1996. *Epicarmo de Siracusa: Testimonios y Fragmentos*. Oviedo.

Roisman, H. 2005. *Sophocles: Philoctetes*. London.

van Rooy, C. A. 1965. *Studies in Classical Satire and Related Literary Theory*. Leiden.

Rosen, R. 2003. 'Sophocles' *Poimenes* Revisited: Tragedy or Satyr Play?' in Sommerstein 2003, 373–86.

Rossi, L. E. 1971. 'Il Ciclope di Euripide come *KOMOS* "mancato"', *Maia* 23: 10–38.

Rossi, L. E. 1972. 'Il dramma satiresco attico. Forma, fortuna e funzione di un genere letterario antico', *Dialoghi di archeologia* 6: 248–301. (pp. 259–81 Reprinted in Seidensticker, 1989, 222–51).

Rubel, A. 2014. *Fear and Loathing in Ancient Athens: Religion and Politics during the Peloponnesian War*. London.

Rusten, J. 2006. 'Who "Invented" Comedy? The Ancient Candidates for the Origins of Comedy and the Visual Evidence', *American Journal of Philology* 126: 37–66.

Rusten, J. (ed.). 2011. *The Birth of Comedy: Texts, Documents, and Art from Athenian Comic Competitions, 486–280*. (trans. J. Henderson, D. Konstan, R. Rosen, J. Rusten, and N. Slater). Baltimore, MD.

Saïd, S. 2011. *Homer and the Odyssey*. Oxford.

Scodel, R. 2017. 'The Euripidean Biography', in McClure 2017, 27–41.

Scullion, S. 2002. '"Nothing to Do with Dionysus": Tragedy Misconceived as Ritual', *Classical Quarterly* 52: 102–37.

Seaford, R. 1976. 'On the Origins of Satyric Drama', *Maia* 28: 209–21.

Seaford, R. 1977–1978. 'The Hyporchema of Pratinas', *Maia* 29–30: 81–94.

Seaford, R. 1981. 'Dionysiac Drama and Dionysiac Mysteries', *Classical Quarterly* 31: 252–75.

Seaford, R. 1982. 'The Date of Euripides' *Cyclops*', *Journal of Hellenic Studies* 102: 161–72.

Seaford, R. 1984. *Euripides Cyclops* (Edited with Introduction and Commentary). Oxford.

Seaford, R. 1987. 'Silenus Erectus: Euripides, *Cyclops* 227', *Liverpool Classical Monthly* 12.9: 142–43.

Seaford, R. 1994. *Reciprocity and Ritual. Homer and Tragedy in the Developing City-State*. Oxford.

Seaford, R. 1996. 'Something to Do with Dionysos—Tragedy and the Dionysiac: Response to Friedrich', in Silk 1996, 284–94.

Seaford, R. 2007. 'From Ritual to Drama: A Concluding Statement', in Csapo and Miller 2007, 379–401.

Segal, C. 1997. *Dionysiac Poetics and Euripides' Bacchae*. Princeton, NJ, expanded edn., originally published Princeton, 1982.

Seidensticker, B. 1989. *Satyrspiel*. Darmstadt.

Seidensticker, B. 2003. 'The Chorus of Greek Satyrplay', in Csapo and Miller 2003, 100–21.

Seidensticker, B. 2010. 'Dance in Satyr Play', in Taplin and Wyles 2010, 213–30.

Seidensticker, B. 2012. 'The Satyr Plays of Sophocles', in *Brill's Companion to Sophocles*, ed. A. Markantonatos, 211–44. Leiden.

Shaw, C. A. 2014. *Satyric Play: The Evolution of Greek Comedy and Satyr Drama*. Oxford.

Shaw, C. A. 2014a. '"Genitalia of the Sea": Seafood and Sexuality in Greek Comedy', *Mnemosyne* 67: 554–76.

Shaw, C. A. Forthcoming. 'Satyrs, Dolphins, Dithyramb and Drama', in *Brill's Companion to Satyr Drama*, ed. A. P. Antonpoulos, G. W. M. Harrison and M. M. Christopoulos. Leiden.

Slater, N. W. 2005. 'Nothing to do with Satyrs? Alcestis and the Concept of Prosatyric Drama', in Harrison 2005, 83–101.

Slater, N. W. 2013 *Euripides: Alcestis*. London.

Slenders, W. 2005. 'Λέξις ἐρωτική in Euripides' Cyclops', in Harrison 2005b, 39–52.

Small, J. P. 2013 'Skenographia in Brief', in Harrison and Liapis 2013, 111–30.

Smith, D. 2004. 'Thucydides' Ignorant Athenians and the Drama of the Sicilian Expedition', *SyllClass* 15: 33–70.

Smith, T. J. 2007. 'The Corpus of Komast Vases. From Identity to Exegesis', in Csapo and Miller 2007, 48–76.

Sommerstein, A. 2008. *Aeschylus Fragments*. Cambridge, MA.

Sommerstein, A. 1986. 'The Decree of Syrakosios', *Classical Quarterly* 36: 101–8.

Sourvinou-Inwood, C. 2003. *Tragedy and Athenian Religion*. Oxford.

Steffen, V. 1971. 'The Satyr Dramas of Euripides', *Eos* 59: 203–26.

Steinhart, M. 2004. *Die Kunst der Nachahmung: Darstellungen mimetischer Vorführungen in der griechischen Bildkunst archaischer und klassischer Zeit*. Mainz.

Steinhart, M. 2007. 'From Ritual to Narrative', in Csapo and Miller 2007, 196–220.

Stewart, A. S. 1997. *Art, the Body, and Desire in Ancient Greece*. Cambridge.

Storey, I. C. 2005. 'But Comedy has Satyrs Too', in G. W. M. Harrison 2005b, 201–18.

Storey, I. C. 2011. *Fragments of Old Comedy*. Cambridge, MA.

Strauss Clay, J. 1983. *The Wrath of Athena: Gods and Men in the* Odyssey. Lanham, MD.

Sutton, D. F. 1974. 'Satyr Plays and the *Odyssey*', *HSCP* 78: 107–43.

Sutton, D. F. 1980. *The Greek Satyr Play*. Meisenheim am Glan.

Tanner, R. 1915. 'The Ὀδυσσῆς of Cratinus and Cyclops of Euripides', *Transactions of the American Philological Association* 46: 173–206.

Taplin, O. 1977. *The Stagecraft of Aeschylus*. Oxford.

Taplin, O. 1985. *Greek Tragedy in Action*. London.

Taplin, O. 2007. *Pots and Plays: Interactions between Tragedy and Greek Vase-Painting of the Fourth Century B.C.* Los Angeles, CA.

Taplin, O. and R. Wyles (eds.). 2010. *The Pronomos Vase and Its Context*. Oxford.

Tillyard, E. M. W. 1923. *The Hope Vases: A Catalogue, and a Discussion of the Hope Collection of Greek Vases, with an Introduction on the History of the Collection, and on Late Attic and South Italian Vases*. Cambridge.

Torrance, I. 2013 *Metapoetry in Euripides*. Oxford and New York.

Trendall, A. D. 1989. *Red Figure Vases of South Italy and Sicily: A Handbook*. London.

Ussher, R. G. 1978. *Euripides: Cyclops*. Rome.

Voelke, P. 2001. *Un théâtre de la marge. Aspects figuratifs et configurationnels du drame satyrique dans l'Athènes classique*. Bari.

West, M. L. 1982. *Greek Metre*. Oxford.

Wetzel, W. 1965. *De Euripidis Fabula Satyrica quae Cyclops Inscribitur cum Homerico Comparata Exemplo.* Wiesbaden.

Whitmarsh, T. 2016. *Battling the Gods: Atheism in the Ancient World.* New York.

Willi, A. 2008. *Sikelismos. Sprache, Literatur und Gesellschaft im griechischen Sizilien (8.-5-Jh. v. Chr.).* Basel.

Wilson, P. 2000. *The Athenian Institution of the Khoregia: The Chorus, The City and the Stage.* Cambridge.

Wilson, P. (ed.). 2007. *The Greek Theatre and Festivals.* Oxford.

Winkler, J. J. and F. I. Zeitlin (eds.). 1990. *Nothing to Do with Dionysus?* Princeton, NJ.

Wiseman, T. P. 1988. 'Satyrs in Rome? The Background to Horace's Ars Poetica', *Journal of Roman Studies* 78: 1–13.

Worman, N. 2002. 'Euripides, Ingestive Rhetoric, and Euripides' *Cyclops*', *Helios* 29: 101–25.

Worman, N. 2008. *Abusive Mouths in Classical Athens.* Cambridge.

Wright, M. 2005. *Euripides' Escape-Tragedies: A Study of Helen, Andromeda, and Iphigenia among the Taurians.* Oxford.

Wright, M. 2006. 'Cyclops and the Euripidean Tetralogy', *Proceedings of the Cambridge Philological Society* 51: 23–48.

Wright, M. 2012. *The Comedian as Critic: Greek Old Comedy and Poetics.* London.

Wright, M. 2016. *The Lost Plays of Greek Tragedy. Volume 1: Neglected Authors.* London.

Xanthakis-Karamanos, G. 1997. 'Echoes of Earlier Drama in Sositheus and Lycophron', *L'Antiqitué classique* 66: 121–43.

Zimmermann, B. 1992. *Dithyrambos: Geschichte einer Gattung.* Göttingen.

Zuntz, G. 1965. An inquiry into the transmission of the plays of Euripides. Cambridge.

van Zyl Smit, B. 2016. *A Handbook to the Reception of Greek Drama.* Chichester, West Sussex.

Index